# CULTURE SMART!
# CUBA

Mandy Macdonald

·K·U·P·E·R·A·R·D·

ISBN 978 1 85733 338 1
This book is also available as an e-book: eISBN 978 1 85733 578 1

British Library Cataloguing in Publication Data
A CIP catalogue entry for this book is available from the
British Library

Copyright © 2006 Kuperard
**Revised 2006, third printing 2011**

First published in Great Britain 2006
by Kuperard, an imprint of Bravo Ltd
59 Hutton Grove, London N12 8DS
Tel: +44 (0) 20 8446 2440   Fax: +44 (0) 20 8446 2441
www.culturesmart.co.uk
Inquiries: sales@kuperard.co.uk

Distributed in the United States and Canada
by Random House Distribution Services
1745 Broadway, New York, NY 10019
Tel: +1 (212) 572-2844   Fax: +1 (212) 572-4961
Inquiries: csorders@randomhouse.com

Series Editor  Geoffrey Chesler
Design  Bobby Birchall

Printed in Malaysia

Cover image: 1950s Chevrolet in front of the Museo de la Revolución, Havana.
*Travel Ink/Charlie Marsden*

## About the Author

MANDY MACDONALD is an Australian writer, researcher, editor, and translator living in Scotland. A graduate of Sydney and Cambridge Universities, she specializes in international affairs with a particular emphasis on Latin American development issues and gender equality. She has lived and worked in Cuba as a translator and has written articles and books on Cuba and Central America.

The Culture Smart! series is continuing to expand.
For further information and latest titles visit
**www.culturesmart.co.uk**

The publishers would like to thank **CultureSmart!**Consulting for its help in researching and developing the concept for this series.

**CultureSmart!**Consulting creates tailor-made seminars and consultancy programs to meet a wide range of corporate, public-sector, and individual needs. Whether delivering courses on multicultural team building in the USA, preparing Chinese engineers for a posting in Europe, training call-center staff in India, or raising the awareness of police forces to the needs of diverse ethnic communities, it provides essential, practical, and powerful skills worldwide to an increasingly international workforce.

For details, visit www.culturesmartconsulting.com

**CultureSmart!**Consulting and **CultureSmart!** guides have both contributed to and featured regularly in the weekly travel program "Fast Track" on BBC World TV.

# contents

# contents

# Map of Cuba

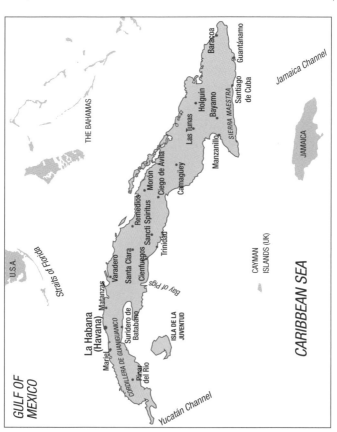

# introduction

Cuba is extensively written about, and from a very broad spectrum of political opinion, of which the loudest and most inflexible voices are heard at the extremes. I hope in this little guide to steer a course between the rock of uncritical support for Fidel Castro's government and the hard place of U.S.–based Cuban exiles' hatred of it. What is undeniable is that Cuba is endlessly fascinating and full of contradictions: a poor country with one of the best health care systems in the world, a developing country with almost 100 percent literacy; and—as many commentators point out—one of the few countries in the world to have seen off three imperial powers: Spain, the United States, and the Soviet Union.

To a great extent, the country is symbolized by its president, commander-in-chief, and *máximo líder*, Fidel Castro, and he is inevitably central to any account of Cuba. Surrounded by speculation and the source of endless anecdotes, he excites ferocious loyalty, entrenched hatred, and pretty much every emotion in between—the only common factor is that you can't ignore him. It is now widely believed that he will leave office only when he is carried out; but he will leave in place a government and a political class run no longer by superannuated revolutionaries but by a new generation of young, university-educated, competent politicians and administrators who have been groomed for government over the years.

In this book you will find chapters on the history and the values that together make Cuba the unique mixture of cultural vibrancy and political intransigence it is today. We look at what everyday life is like for Cubans, how they celebrate on special occasions, and how you can meet Cubans outside the tourist enclaves. We offer some hints on traveling around the country, on activities beyond the beach that you can enjoy as a visitor, and on doing business in Cuba.

Cuba is a great deal more than its controversial system of government. It is physically beautiful and seductive, and it has a rich and ever-evolving culture that existed long before the revolution of 1959 and will certainly long outlive it. The Cuban people are tough, resilient, egalitarian, and pathologically sociable. At the same time they can be opinionated, self-dramatizing, and sometimes infuriating or exhausting to be with. But they are always generous-spirited and invigorating. In *Culture Smart! Cuba*, we aim to help you get to know them better.

## Key Facts

| | | |
|---|---|---|
| **Official Name** | *República de Cuba* | A member of WTO, ECLAC, UNCTAD, ACP, G-77, NAM, ILO |
| **Capital City** | Havana (La Habana) | Pop. 2.2 million (2005 est.) |
| **Main Cities** | Santiago de Cuba, Camagüey, Trinidad, Santa Clara, Holguín | |
| **Area** | 42,804 sq. miles (110,861 sq. km) | |
| **Climate** | Subtropical | Hurricanes frequent August–October |
| **Population** | 11.35 million (2005 est.) | Population growth rate 0.33% |
| **Ethnic Makeup** | In 1990, 51% mulatto (mixed-race Spanish/African), 37% white, 11% black, 1% Chinese | |
| **Languages** | Spanish | |
| **Religion** | Largest Christian group is Roman Catholic. A number of Protestant churches are present, plus Quakers, Jehovah's Witnesses. There is a small Jewish community. | Many Cubans practice the animistic Yoruba religion known in Cuba as *santería* or the Regla de Oshá, or related African religions. |
| **Government** | One-party state ruled by the Communist Party of Cuba (PCC). Elections to the National Assembly are held every five years. | |

| | | |
|---|---|---|
| **Currency** | Peso. The U.S. dollar made legal currency 1993; convertible peso (CUC) introduced 1995, replaced dollar for most purposes in 2004. | Neither the Cuban peso nor the CUC can be used outside Cuba. The CUC has approximate parity with the U.S. dollar. |
| **Media** | Daily newspapers: *Granma*, *Juventud Rebelde*, *Trabajadores*. Several weeklies and magazines | Three national TV channels; seven national radio stations. All media are state-controlled. |
| **Media: English-language** | *Granma International*, weekly published in English and several other languages. *Cartelera*, bilingual cultural weekly | |
| **Electricity** | 110 volts, 60 Hz. Some hotels also have 220 volt supply. | Most sockets take plugs with two flat or round pins. Electrical fittings often in poor condition; care recommended. |
| **Video/TV** | Videos use the NTSC system. | |
| **Internet Domain** | .cu | |
| **Telephone** | Cuba's country code is 53. There are area codes for provinces and cities. | For direct-dialed calls out of Cuba, dial 119. Numbers often change. Many calls are made by operator. |
| **Time Zone** | Standard time is 5 hours behind GMT. | Daylight saving time, March to October: GMT -4 |

# LAND & PEOPLE

## GEOGRAPHICAL SNAPSHOT

Long and lissom, the island of Cuba lies in the turquoise Caribbean like a sleeping crocodile, Cubans say. It is the largest island of the Greater Antilles, guarding the mouth of the Gulf of Mexico, just 112 miles (180 km) from Florida and 130 miles (210 km) from Mexico. Cuba is really an archipelago consisting of the long main island, the small Isle of Youth (Isla de la Juventud) off the southwest coast, and about 1,600 coastal islets, keys, and coral reefs. The total surface area is 42,805 sq. miles (110,861 sq. km)—about the size of England, and slightly smaller than the state of Pennsylvania. The mainland is 776 miles (1,250 km) long and 62 miles (100 km) wide.

Cuba is largely low-lying, with a flat or gently undulating landscape of farms, sugar plantations, wetlands, and forested hills. The three chief mountain ranges are the eastern Sierra Maestra, which contains Cuba's highest peak, Pico Turquino (6,476 ft/1,974 m), the Sierra del Escambray in central Cuba, and the Cordillera de

Guaniguanico in the west. Characteristic of the western landscape are *mogotes*, steep-sided, rounded limestone hills rearing up straight out of the plain. Only a few rivers are navigable. About 4 percent of the main island is wetlands; the most important is the Zapata Swamp, in the southwest.

About 14 percent of Cuba's landmass is protected in national and local reserves, including fourteen national parks. Seven protected areas are designated as UNESCO biosphere reserves, including one near Baracoa in the eastern province of Guantánamo (which includes Cuba's longest river, the Río de Miel) and the 80,060-acre (32,400-hectare) Parque Baconoa, the largest reserve, near Santiago de Cuba.

Cuba has fourteen provinces, including the capital, plus a special municipality, the Isle of Youth. About one-fifth of the population of 11.35 million lives in Havana.

## CLIMATE

Cuba has a tropical marine climate, with temperatures averaging between around 71° and 80°F (around 22° and 27°C). Because of its narrow east-west configuration, it is refreshed by sea breezes and trade winds, but daytime temperatures can rise to around 97°F (36°C) in July and August and inland in the east of the island. Conversely, between December and February, although the average temperature is around 68°F (20°C), cold fronts can sweep down from the north, bringing rain and sudden sharp temperature drops.

February and March are the driest months and October the wettest month. Average annual rainfall is around 52 inches (1,320 mm), the highest rainfalls occurring in the mountains and the lowest along the coastline south of them. At any time of year, the weather can switch from glorious sunshine to a torrential downpour and back to

sunshine again in an hour or two. As the wet season begins, temperature and humidity rise together, and the beach becomes a place of refuge with the sea temperature topping 77°F (25°C).

**The Hurricane**

Cuba lies in the Caribbean's "Hurricane Avenue." Hurricanes generally coincide with the wet season and are most frequent between August and October. On average, Cuba is affected by a hurricane about every three years, with a direct hit every eight or nine years. The most recent hurricanes were Charley in August 2004 and Dennis in July 2005—the first recorded occurrence of direct hits in two successive years.

Cuba's hurricane preparedness is efficient. Emergency procedures are posted in all hotels and in other public places, and broadcast on radio. All modern hotels are built to withstand hurricanes, and the older hotels have been reinforced.

## A BRIEF HISTORY

When the last consignments of preferentially priced Cuban sugar were delivered to Soviet ports in 1990–91, Cuba sank into a deep economic trough from which it is only now emerging. But at that moment—although Cubans hardly saw it as a victory at the time—the country was for the first time in its history completely independent of any great power. This brief account traces Cuba's long walk to true, if challenging, independence.

### Origins and Conquest

The first inhabitants of Cuba were the Guanajatabeyes, who were hunters and fishers migrating from the northern coasts of the South American mainland, possibly around 2500 BCE. They were later pushed to the western end of the island by the arrival of two Arawak Indian groups, the Siboneys and the Taínos, who appear to have brought a more sophisticated material culture based on agriculture.

These people's enjoyment of the island Columbus thought the most beautiful place ever seen was brought to an abrupt end by his arrival there in October 1492. Cuba was Columbus's second landfall in America, and he went to his grave believing it to be part of a continent. From about 1510, under Diego Velázquez de Cuéllar, the island was annexed by Spain and claimed for the Roman Catholic faith—although to Bartolomé de las Casas, the Spanish priest who recorded the eradication of the native peoples with horror in his *History of the Indies*, the violent conquest of the Indians' lands was "far . . . from the purpose of God and His Church." The conquered people were coerced into labor on the lands they had lost. By 1515 most of today's main towns existed.

An insurrection led by the indigenous chieftain Hatuey, who was captured and burned at the stake in 1511 or 1512, has become symbolic of Cuban indigenous resistance. But by the mid-sixteenth century most of the Taínos had either been killed or had melted away into the mountains, where they possibly held out for many generations, even into the twentieth century.

## Plunder and Piracy

In the sixteenth and seventeenth centuries Spain used Cuba first as a launching pad for fresh conquests and then as an entrepôt for its trade with the Americas. The conquerors soon realized the strategic value of Cuba's location at the gateway to the Gulf of Mexico not only for trade but also for defending their new empire against the French, Dutch, and English.

From Cuba itself the Spanish exported fine woods, leather, citrus fruits, tobacco and—increasingly—sugar, grown by slave labor on large plantations. The first evidence of African slaves in Cuba dates from 1513, and by the seventeenth century the slave trade was well established. This increasingly lively commerce, together with constant military activity in the seas around the Americas, attracted the attention of pirates and privateers, who did much damage to coastal towns. Francis Drake was among them, his fleet standing off Cuba in 1589.

Spain made no attempt to develop Cuba's own economy, however: everything was grown for export, and colonists were prohibited by law from developing their own industries and commerce or from trading with any power other than Spain. This economic powerlessness was to persist right up to the 1950s, when 75 percent of the country's

agricultural land was in foreign—mostly U.S.—
hands. However, Havana prospered as a city of
commerce and entertainment.

## A Brief British Occupation
In 1762 a large British armed fleet captured
Havana, as part of a British offensive against
Spain at the end of the Seven Years' War
(1756–63). The British invaders immediately
opened up trade between Cuba and Britain and
its North American possessions. Within a year,
however, Cuba and the Philippines were returned
to the Spanish in exchange for Florida by the
Treaty of Paris in 1763. Unfortunately, the most
lasting effect was a sharp escalation in the slave
trade with Africa.

## Sugar Dependency
As the demand for sugar in Europe and North
America soared, Cuba was ready to supply it. By
1827 it was the world's major producer, and sugar
was to remain Cuba's principal export for nearly
two hundred years. But production required

massive slave labor. As slavery ended in Santo Domingo (today's Dominican Republic) in 1791 and Haiti in 1803, exiled slave owners flocked to eastern Cuba. The advent of steam power and railways in the mid-nineteenth century accelerated production and profit but made life even harsher for the slaves and other workers.

The early nineteenth century saw many Latin American countries win independence from Spain, but not Cuba—Spain's profits from Cuba were too great. Since the previous century the *criollo* (creole) planters, born in Cuba of Spanish origin, had been resenting the colonial power, wanting property rights and the right to develop their own capital. The mid-century emigration of poor Spaniards to Cuba and growing trade with the United States made this call both louder and more rational. But Spain clung fiercely to its cash cow, and it was not until 1878 that it conceded even promises of reform and greater autonomy.

**Breaking Away from Spain**

The Ten Years' War (1868–78) was ignited when, in October 1868, Manuel de Céspedes, a *criollo* planter, freed all the slaves on his small plantation at La Demajagua and called for independence from Spain in a speech known to every Cuban as *el Grito de Yara* (the Cry of Yara). Thousands of freed slaves, peasants, and indentured laborers flocked to Céspedes's rebel army, headed in the field by Máximo Gómez and Antonio Maceo. As  the Spanish brought in more and more soldiers, the rebels, calling themselves *mambises* after Juan Mambí, a Dominican freedom fighter, turned successfully to guerrilla warfare. After Céspedes's death in 1874, a stalemate in 1878 led to the Pact of Zanjón, whereby the landowners and the Spanish agreed on some reforms. Slavery was finally abolished in 1886; but Cuba was still Spanish, and insurrection smoldered on.

In 1894 Spain cancelled a trade agreement between the United States and Cuba, precipitating a fresh war in 1895. The rebels sabotaged the sugar industry and Spanish property, and the Spain retaliated by driving the rural population into concentration camps, where thousands died. The rebellion was led again by Gómez and Maceo, under the political inspiration of José Martí (see box). In 1897 Spain offered Cuba autonomy, but the rebels insisted on full independence.

The final chapter was played out in the brief Spanish-American War (1898), which erupted when an American battleship, USS *Maine*, blew up in mysterious circumstances in Havana harbor on February 15. Congress declared war on Spain on April 21; U.S. forces won swift victories in eastern Cuba, and a treaty was signed in April 1899 giving the United States Cuba, Puerto Rico, Guam, and the Philippines.

### JOSÉ MARTÍ, NATIONAL HERO

Born in Havana in 1853, José Martí was one of Latin America's greatest journalists and writers. He was an internationalist, and argued strongly for racial equality. But it was his political activism that made him Cuba's national hero during the second war of independence. As an exile in the United States, he mobilized support for independence among other Cuban exiles. He was also the first to warn of the danger the U.S.A. represented to Cuba, as U.S. companies moved into the Cuban sugar industry once slavery ended. He was shot and killed early in the uprising. In contrast to public images of Castro, which are rare, Martí's image appears everywhere in Cuba, both outside and inside schools, hospitals, and government offices—even on the one-peso note.

**The Pseudo-Republic**

The defeat of Spain did not mean independence for Cuba, however. Spanish rule was effectively replaced by U.S. rule—military occupation until 1902, and thereafter *de facto* rule by virtue of the Platt Amendment, an agreement between the United States and Cuba that gave the United States the power to intervene at any time "for the preservation of Cuban independence [and] the maintenance of a government adequate for the protection of life, property and individual liberty." The Amendment enabled the United States to acquire the naval base at Guantánamo in 1903, and was used to justify four U.S. interventions in Cuba before its repeal in 1934.

By 1902 Cuba was nominally independent under its first president, Tomás Estrada Palma. However, broken by war, with most of its population poor, illiterate, and in ill health, it was utterly dependent on the United States, which made no more effort to develop it than Spain had done. The sugar industry was

modernized and mechanized but became a monopoly serving only the interests of the United States, the main market for Cuban sugar and the main investor in the industry. By the mid-1920s,

U.S. companies controlled two-thirds of Cuban agriculture. The sugar boom of the 1920s paid for imposing public buildings and luxurious houses for the wealthy but gave nothing to the poor. U.S. companies built roads and railways and installed banks, electricity, and the world's first automated telephone system, but repatriated all the profits.

Not surprisingly, the Cuban government had little political power or authority. Corruption bloomed, particularly under General Gerardo Machado (1925–33), while opposition from the labor movement and the political left was mercilessly repressed. Influenced by the ideas and propagandists of the Russian Revolution, the Cuban Communist Party was founded in 1925 and became strong in the labor movement.

Into this society Fidel Castro was born on August 13, 1926.

**The Rise of Batista**

In 1933 massive opposition to Machado's government culminated in a general strike, and Machado fled into exile. Into the ensuing political confusion, which included a progressive but extremely short-lived government headed by Ramón Grau San Martín and Antonio Guiteras, stepped Fulgencio Batista, a young mulatto army officer, who seized power in January 1934.

Batista, a slippery operator loyal only to himself, was to retain his power and influence in one way or another for the next fifteen years, supported by both the U.S. government and the Mafia. In 1940, he brought in a new constitution that promoted labor rights, a minimum wage, and even equal pay for equal work, and cooperated with the Communist Party when he found it expedient. Losing the 1944 elections, he withdrew to Florida, leaving Cuba practically ungovernable. Returning in 1952 just before the presidential elections, he carried out a bloodless coup, beginning a violent, crime-ridden, seven-year dictatorship. Havana became famous as a decadent American playground, while the corpses appearing daily on the streets of Santiago bore gruesome witness to the price of opposition.

**From Moncada to the Sierra Maestra**
The rebel attack on the Moncada barracks in Santiago de Cuba on July 26, 1953, can be considered the beginning of Cuba's revolution.

Fidel Castro had already begun building a movement to overthrow Batista, principally among radicals in the left-wing Ortodoxo Party, formed in 1947, to which he belonged at the

time. The capture of the Moncada barracks, the country's second-most important garrison, was intended to set off a popular uprising throughout the country. But the rebels were outnumbered and soon overpowered. Many were tortured to death, and Castro and twenty-eight others were imprisoned. Released in May 1955 in an amnesty, they promptly resumed their struggle under a new organization, the 26 July Movement.

Before long, Fidel left for Mexico to plan his campaign, as Martí had done, from exile. There he met the young Argentinian doctor Ernesto Guevara, known to his friends—and now to the world—as "Che." On November 25, 1956, after months of planning and fund-raising, eighty-two revolutionaries embarked for Cuba in bad weather in an old, leaky motorboat, the *Granma*. Running aground in dense mangrove swamps, they were immediately decimated by Batista's troops. Just twelve of them reached the Sierra Maestra, from where they slowly gained the trust and support of the local peasants, built up a guerrilla army, and began to win clashes with Batista's troops. The Sierra was also a learning experience for many of the revolutionaries in understanding firsthand the lives of the peasants.

As the guerrillas gained control, Batista sent more and more soldiers to the Sierra, but to no avail. Other guerrilla groups sprang up around

### *FIDEL, FIGURE OF LEGEND*

Fidel Castro is the world's longest-serving head of government, despite the many, frequently bizarre, plots to kill him. Charismatic but elusive, he is practically impossible to meet by appointment, though he will suddenly make an appearance or grant an audience without notice, sailing through a roomful of people surrounded by a shoal of functionaries and guards. His loquacity, omnivorous and idiosyncratic interest, and breadth of knowledge are legendary. Among hundreds of speeches and pamphlets, *History will absolve me*, Fidel's speech at his trial for the Moncada attempt, is his most impressive, a passionate polemic against the Batista regime and a detailed denunciation of the plight of the poor.

Whether history absolves him or not, and whether his refusal to compromise on his own political ideals is seen by posterity as admirable or boneheaded, Fidel certainly cannot be dismissed as a doctrinaire Communist. The model of socialism he has developed in Cuba, itself continually evolving, owes as much to the ideas of Martí and Che as to Marx and Lenin, and is to a large extent Fidel's own creation.

the island. After a battle at Jigüe in May 1958, Batista's soldiers, demoralized, abandoned the Sierra. As the rebel force advanced westward and Che Guevara captured a troop train near Santa Clara in December, Batista's army collapsed. On January 1, 1959, Batista left for Santo Domingo, and a week later the revolutionaries entered Havana in triumph. Fidel was thirty-two years old, Che thirty, and they had a country to run.

## Revolution

The first months of the Revolution were dizzying. Although the moderates Manuel Urrutia and José Miró Cardona were appointed president and prime minister, the "Granma group"—Fidel, his brother Raúl, Che Guevara, and a few others—were really at the helm. The brothels and casinos were closed, the long-awaited agrarian reform was initiated, racial equality was declared and all whites-only restrictions removed, rents were reduced and tenants given rights, and new ministries were formed to oversee the reforms—including the expropriation of the properties of Batista and his cronies and, increasingly, U.S.-owned businesses. The sugar mills were nationalized by February 1960.

## The Empire Strikes Back

These radical changes laid the foundation for the hostile standoff between the U.S. and Cuba that has endured ever since. While the Cuban poor were jubilant, the U.S. government was quick to react. As early as March 1959, it was secretly planning to overthrow Castro.

When the first shipment of Soviet crude oil in exchange for sugar arrived in Cuba in April 1960, U.S. companies in Cuba, under pressure from their government, refused to refine it, so Fidel expropriated them. When the U.S. retaliated by cutting its sugar import quota, the Soviet Union bought up the unsold sugar. In November, the U.S. declared a trade embargo. Although the Soviet bloc helped plug the import gap, the embargo—still in force today—created much hardship and drove the Cuban economy into a different dependence that would be exposed when the Soviet bloc itself disintegrated.

**Economic Reform**

Serious economic reform began in 1961. Che Guevara, in charge of the process, was an original thinker but not an economist or a manager. His ideas were radical and utopian, and many proved impossible to carry out. But Che also saw the need to diversify the island's economy away from the sugar monoculture. There was much debate about industrialization, but there were few trained economists left in Cuba. The new rulers had not realized the true cost of redistributing national wealth massively to the rural poor and ignoring the interests of educated urban professionals. Industrial expertise drained away, and the U.S. embargo blocked access to industrial inputs and impeded the use of existing U.S.-owned infrastructure. Soviet-made replacements of U.S. equipment were less efficient and unfamiliar to the workforce. Given the circumstances, continued reliance on sugar and raw material production was the only realistic option.

The year 1961 saw the national literacy crusade, in which a million Cubans—men and women equally—particularly in remote rural areas, were taught to read and write by 100,000 young volunteer teachers. So bold and successful was this experiment that it caught the imagination of the world and became a defining symbol of the Cuban revolution.

### The Bay of Pigs

However, on April 17, 1961, just as the young teachers were heading for the remotest corners of Cuba with their exercise books and storm lanterns, about 1,400 anti-Castro Cuban exiles, sponsored and supported by the United States, invaded Cuba at the Bay of Pigs (Playa Girón) in the Zapata swamplands. The Cuban army defeated them within forty-eight hours, but from that moment on the country was defined as being in a constant state of military readiness against the United States. Fidel, in his funeral speech for the seven Cuban soldiers killed, for the first time clearly declared the Revolution and the Cuban state socialist.

## The Missile Crisis

A year later, Cuba became the theater for one of the most alarming incidents of the Cold War, when Castro allowed the Soviet Union to deploy nuclear missiles on Cuban soil. A launch site was constructed and warheads had actually begun arriving when the U.S. imposed a naval  blockade on Cuba. They were withdrawn, but the world came breathtakingly close to nuclear war. The decision to stand down was made in a blizzard of letters between presidents Kennedy and Khrushchev, showing how easy it was for a small country to become a pawn in the deadly East–West power game.

## In the Soviet Fold

Throughout the rest of the 1960s and the 1970s Cuba drew closer to the Soviet bloc and Cuban

Communism was at its most orthodox. The Communist Party was restructured along stricter Marxist–Leninist lines as the *Partido Comunista de Cuba* (PCC) in 1965 and held its first Congress in 1975. In 1976, under the provisions of the new constitution introduced that year, the National Assembly of People's Power, the Cuban parliament, was established.

This was an unhappy period for intellectual life: civil rights were restricted, university departments were closed down, and writers and artists could not publish even mild criticism of the socialist system. Though much art, literature, and particularly film was produced, the cultural adventurousness of the Revolution's earliest years was diluted, especially after 1968. In that year, Castro resoundingly criticized Alexander Dubcek's "Prague Spring" and outlawed small family businesses, the last remnants of private enterprise at home.

This was also the period of "exporting revolution" to other Third World countries. Cuba became involved in armed revolutionary struggles, for example in Nicaragua and Grenada, and in support to Soviet-backed regimes such as Ethiopia. From 1976 Cuban troops played a key role in Angola's civil war, defeating the South African forces at Cuito Cuanavale in 1988.

## *La Rectificación*

In 1986 Castro launched a process called "rectification," declaring that the Revolution needed to return to socialist ethical values, moral incentives—and more efficient central planning. Meetings with the population were held over an entire year. Fidel stated on July 26, 1987, that rectification was "not idealism, but realism, better use of the economic management and planning system," and a correction of deviations "from the revolutionary spirit, from revolutionary work, revolutionary virtue, revolutionary effort, revolutionary responsibility."

Typical of this approach was the abrupt closure, in May 1986, of the private farmers' and craft markets that had been allowed to open in the early 1980s, on the grounds that they were enticements to undue individual enrichment. Volunteer work brigades, used to good effect in the 1970s to confront housing shortages, were reintroduced, and the bureaucracy was slimmed down by many thousands in 1988.

## The Soviet Collapse and the Special Period

In 1989 the Berlin wall fell and the world changed. Over the next few years Soviet aid and subsidies were withdrawn from Cuba and the countries of the disappearing "Eastern bloc" redirected their trade. As these props fell away, the

Cuban government launched a severe austerity regime with the Orwellian title of "Special Period in Peacetime," aiming to keep the country afloat without caving in to the embargo or endangering Cuba's social achievements. Limited market-oriented reforms were made, mostly in agriculture and tourism. Cuba desperately sought new export products (sugar by-products, pharmaceuticals, and high-tech medical equipment) and new trading partners, and strove for self-sufficiency in food production and medical products. But fuel and other shortages soon made themselves felt: the transportation system collapsed, power outages (cuts) became a daily irritant, and the lines at shops grew longer as the shelves got barer.

The Fourth Party Congress, in 1991, was unusually open and consultative and introduced some democratic reforms, such as secret ballots—though there was no talk of abandoning the one-party system. Greater powers were given to the elected National Assembly and several members of the revolutionary Old Guard were replaced with promising young Communists. Religious believers were admitted to the Party. Redefining isolation as independence, the leadership increasingly emphasized the homegrown nature of Cuban socialism. "No one gave us a revolution,"

Fidel told journalists in April 1990. "It wasn't imported from anywhere: we made it ourselves."

**Exile the Cuban Way**

Fighting for change in Cuba from somewhere else is a traditional Cuban form of protest: both José Martí and Fidel Castro employed it, and the anti-Castro Cuban exile community in the United States is among the most powerful pressure groups in the world (though it has not really managed to change anything in Cuba).

Apart from a steady trickle of "defectors," exodus on a grand scale has taken place twice since the early mass departures. In 1980, after a dialogue between Castro and Miami Cubans on the phased release of political prisoners and visits to Cuba by Cubans living abroad, thousands stormed the Peruvian embassy in Havana demanding asylum. Castro decided to allow people to leave from the port of Mariel. More than 100,000 did so before both countries replaced migration controls.

In 1994, thousands more left on small boats and rafts in response to the hardships of the Special Period, prompting a sea change in U.S. policy toward Cuban migration allowing for controlled migration (20,000 visas a year) and the repatriation of Cuban "boat people" ineligible for political asylum.

## Independent at Last?

By 1993 the economic crisis was deep. After exhaustive nationwide discussions, a series of reforms was introduced that effectively reshaped the Cuban economy: making the U.S. dollar legal tender in Cuba, enabling (and taxing) self-employment, replacing the old state farms with cooperatives and enabling the return of the farmers' markets, and extending the legislation governing joint ventures with foreign investors.

The U.S. response was to tighten the embargo by bolstering existing legislation seeking to prevent third parties from trading with Cuba, such as the 1996 Helms–Burton Act (see below, page 47). None the less, the economic crisis bottomed out and recovery began, based on the recognition that Cuba's survival depends on its coming to terms with the international economy and finding its place in it. At present, that place is as a tourist destination. The 1997 Party Congress called for an expansion of tourism, and in 2002, the government officially abandoned sugar as the country's chief earner.

The Congress did not match economic with political liberalization, however, but continued to defend the one-party system. Nowadays the government promotes an image of modernity and nationalism, emphasizing Cuba's successes in the teeth of U.S. hostility rather than the virtues of Communism. Pope John Paul II, visiting the island in January 1998, implicitly praised Cuba for not taking the neoliberal capitalist road at the expense of its poor, while urging the regime to allow freedom of belief, "the basis of all other human rights." In response Castro publicly recognized the Church, which had been suppressed since the early 1960s, and allowed services, baptisms, and an increase in the clergy. However, Cuba continues to attract international criticism over its human rights record. Speculation about the post-Castro future is Cuba-watchers' favorite game, but in fact Fidel has gradually withdrawn from hands-on government and a new generation of leaders is running the country in practice. Whether there is further political opening up or not may well depend on the reaction of the United States and key European governments to the end of the Castro era. Gradually, and rather quietly, Cuba is learning to live with its independence.

## THE POLITICAL SYSTEM
### The One-Party State
Cuba is a one-party parliamentary republic, led by the Communist Party of Cuba (PCC). Although the definition of the state as

Marxist–Leninist in the 1976 Constitution was removed in 1992, the PCC is the only legal political party. Party members and citizens involved in the mass organizations are consulted, but the Party makes the final decisions.

The president is both head of state and head of government. Fidel Castro has been president since 1976 (having been prime minister from 1959 until that date, when that office was abolished). He is also president of the Councils of State and Ministers, first secretary of the PCC, commander-in-chief of the armed forces, and the National Assembly representative for Santiago de Cuba. His brother Raúl is first vice president of the Councils of State and Ministers, second secretary of the PCC, and minister of defense.

The thirty-one-member Council of State is elected by the National Assembly to exercise legislative power when the Assembly is not in session. Eight of its members form the Council of Ministers, the cabinet. The Assembly also elects the president.

Castro justifies the one-party state by appealing to the overriding need for unity against U.S. hostility. He believes Cuba would not be able to deal with the U.S. threat so successfully if it were politically divided. In that sense the U.S. stance has hardened Fidel's determination not to allow pluralism. His successors may decide otherwise.

**Parliament and Elections**

The National Assembly of People's Power (*Asamblea Nacional del Poder Popular*) has 609 seats. Its members are elected directly from lists proposed and approved at constituency level. There is universal suffrage from the age of sixteen.

Elections for the 169 municipal assemblies are held every two and a half years, and general (including presidential) elections every five years. By law, the PCC may not nominate candidates, and candidates do not have to be members of the Party, but in practice most of them are. Despite the introduction of the secret ballot in 1991, Fidel Castro was reelected president with the usual near-universal majority in subsequent elections.

**The Mass Organizations**

Early in the revolutionary period mass social organizations were formed to protect the interests of different groups in society. The Federation of Cuban Women (FMC) was created in April 1960, and the Association of Small Farmers (ANAP) in May 1962. Some, such as student organizations and the trade union federation, had already existed for many years and joined the ensemble of revolutionary organizations, though the trade unions in particular were reshaped to serve the needs of the government, which had become the only employer. Most controversial are the Committees for the Defense of the Revolution (CDRs), a national network of neighborhood-level committees created immediately before the Playa Girón incident to be the "eyes and ears of the Revolution" (see page 93). All the mass organizations are still active, and there is evidence that they have some influence on policy.

**What Kind of Socialism?**
Opinions on the nature of Cuban socialism are polarized. Castro himself locates it in a Latin American, not a North American or European, tradition. Although fairly orthodox Soviet-style Communism held sway from the late 1960s to the early '80s, Cuban communism in practice has many specifically Latin American features, not least in the way Castro fits the image of the Latin American *caudillo*, a usually charismatic political-military leader. The nationalist heritage of Martí is very strong, and is increasingly emphasized, and the moralism of Che is also noticeable.

**The Human Rights Situation**
Cuba's human rights record illustrates acutely the contradictions between social equity and political

and social control. Cuba has a system of social provision and protection unequaled among developing countries; yet the government imprisons its critics, practices censorship, and has only recently allowed limited freedom of religion and sexual orientation (though homosexuals are still not allowed to join the Communist Party). There are an estimated 100 to 200 small groups of political dissidents in the country, but probably only about 500 people are really active. Even fewer have a reputation abroad, and their voice is disproportionate to their number. A significant— but unsuccessful—recent attempt to express dissent by legal means was the Varela Project, a petition using constitutional means to demand a referendum on democracy. The government rejected it in 2002.

The latest headline-making crackdown, in 2003, surprised those who thought that the government might be becoming more tolerant of its opponents, with a drop in the number of prisoners of conscience and a *de facto* moratorium on the death penalty since 2000. In early 2005, Amnesty International estimated the number of prisoners of conscience in Cuban jails as seventy-one.

Castro does himself no favors by refusing to cooperate with respected international monitors, but even the most recent human rights delegation, in 1988, admitted that conditions in Cuban prisons were no worse than those in U.S. prisons. Amnesty says that the embargo, and especially U.S. funding for "democracy building" in Cuba, play into the government's hands, enabling it to lump all dissidents together as U.S. sympathizers.

Cuban policy highlights a contradiction between civil and political rights and economic and social rights: since the overriding issue for the Revolution was to overcome long-standing poverty and discrimination, the former rights were not given the same importance as the latter, and U.S. hostility later became the pretext for the curtailment of freedom of expression and organization.

## THE ECONOMY

Cuba's economy is dominated by the state sector. Sugar, the historical linchpin of the economy, is no longer the principal foreign exchange earner, having been replaced by tourism. Other important export commodities are citrus fruit, tobacco, nickel, seafood, medical products, and coffee. Its most vital import is oil.

After an estimated 35 percent contraction in 1990–93, the Cuban economy is now clearly recovering. According to the UN Economic Commission on Latin America and the

Caribbean, the economy grew by 3 percent in 2004, a slight advance on the 2003 figure of 2.6 percent, and probably grew by as much as 5 percent in 2005, helped by tourism and rising production of nickel, oil, and gas.

Remittances from Cubans living abroad also make a noticeable contribution to the economy— about 3 percent, according to some estimates.

The adoption of organic agriculture is a good example of necessity breeding invention. During the Special Period the government encouraged people to grow food and experimented with large-scale organic agriculture. This was so successful that the whole country has been converted to organic production, and it is now the only form of agriculture permitted by law.

**The Rebirth of Trade and Investment**
Foreign trade and investment have grown steadily despite U.S. legislation seeking to stop third parties from trading with Cuba, and it currently trades with many countries, including the U.S.A. Despite the embargo, Cuba has begun receiving significant agricultural imports from the United States, in response to the feeling of many U.S. companies that their own government's policies were depriving them of an attractive market.

Openness to foreign investment began with a law in 1982 permitting joint ventures with Cuban state enterprises, and subsequent legislation in 1995 defined and regulated various forms of economic association with foreign investors. Since the first hotel resulting from a Spanish–Cuban joint venture was built in 1988, over three hundred international economic associations have been created in numerous sectors.

**From Full Employment to Self-Employment**
Self-employment was made legal in 1993. It was intended at least partly to mop up the redundant labor force created by the reduction of both the sugar industry and the state bureaucracy. Self-employment was restricted to family-run businesses and certain activities. Currently there are about 150,000 licensed small entrepreneurs.

Private enterprise opened the way for taxation; personal income tax was introduced in 1996. This was practically unknown to Cubans, and many small businesses, possibly alarmed by its implications, dropped out of the market. Cuba's income tax rate is the highest in Latin America, at 50 percent; corporate tax is lower, at 35 percent.

**The Currency Seesaw**
The U.S. dollar was made legal tender in 1993, formalizing an existing *de facto* dual-currency system. In 1995 the government introduced a third currency, the Cuban convertible peso (*peso*

*convertible*, or CUC), which has approximate parity with the U.S. dollar and is exchangeable for 22 to 26 ordinary Cuban pesos.

Use of the dollar soon led to social divisions between those with access to dollars—through work in tourism or remittances from families abroad, for example—and those without. Possibly because of the weakness of the dollar, it was replaced in domestic retail transactions by the convertible

peso (CUC) in October 2004. It has not been abolished, but simply removed from circulation. However, the change to the CUC has not really restored social equity—there are now CUC haves and have-nots. Beyond the practical implications for visitors (see page 104), it is too early to predict the long-term effect of this policy on the economy.

The most likely development of Cuba's economy is toward a mixed economy with both socialist and capitalist features, striving for economic growth that does not threaten—indeed can finance—the social benefits the Revolution has achieved: a typically pragmatic and inventive Cuban solution.

## CUBA IN THE WORLD
### Cuba and the Third World

From the outset the Revolution aspired to leadership of the poor and oppressed worldwide. The days of support of armed liberation struggles are over, however, and Cuba's internationalism is now expressed in support of anti-U.S. and left-wing governments, development assistance in the form of doctors, teachers, and other professionals, and training for foreign students. Chair of the Non-Aligned Movement embracing developing countries and national liberation movements in the late 1970s, Castro is still respected, particularly in Africa, as a Third World elder statesman and standard-bearer against Western imperialism. Some solidarity efforts, however, such as his support for Robert Mugabe's Zimbabwe, are ill-judged to say the least.

Latin American views on Cuba are not as disapproving as those of the U.S.A. or even European governments. Latin Americans, accustomed to *caudillismo* and fragile or corrupt "democratic" governments, tend to be less dismayed by Fidel's political longevity than those who believe in electoral democracy at any price. The left in Latin America still acknowledges Cuba's social achievements as benchmarks in development. Hence Cuba's flourishing relationship with the government of Hugo Chávez in Venezuela, which supplies Cuba with oil at preferential terms in return for medicines, sugar, and other commodities, and the services of Cuban specialists.

Developing countries have seen how the neoliberalism promoted by the rich world has failed them. Fidel's views are increasingly in tune with today's anticapitalism and antiglobalization movements and he is expert at building on such convergences and reinventing himself as a spokesman for the world's poor. In 2000 Havana hosted the first-ever South Summit of the G77 group of developing countries.

Cuba is a member of the WTO, most UN organizations, and many Latin American ones; in fact, the only important regional organization from which it is formally excluded, at U.S. insistence, is the Organization of American States.

### Cuba and the United States

It seems astonishing that relations between Cuba and the United States have been so bad for so long without coming to outright war. In fact the Cuban government sees itself as permanently at war with the U.S.A. The U.S. embargo has held back Cuban development since its inception; but equally undeniably it has not had the political effect it aimed for. Fidel is still in place, an irritant to successive U.S. governments. Elections are held regularly, but not in a form the U.S. is prepared to countenance. Now and then—usually under Democratic presidencies— "normalization" of relations seems possible, but these openings prove to be temporary. George W. Bush's administration has recently tightened the embargo further.

The rabidly anti-Castro Cuban exile community in the U.S.A. exercises considerable influence on the U.S. government. Recovery of the properties expropriated in the 1960s is one of its perennial preoccupations. The primary aim of the 1996 Helms–Burton Act is to penalize anyone doing business with Cuban enterprises based on confiscated property and to enable former owners to sue for compensation for its loss.

**Cuba and Europe**
European countries and the European Union are valuable counterweights to U.S. policy on Cuba, although human rights issues cause sporadic breaks in diplomatic relations and aid programs.

Despite disapproving of the restrictions on civil and political liberties in Cuba, E.U. member states were quick to capture the Cuban market after the disappearance of Soviet-bloc support, and European businesses have found ways of circumventing Helms–Burton. The E.U. opened a mission in Havana early in 2003, and promptly had to deliver political and cultural snubs (but not economic sanctions) after the arrest of seventy-five opposition figures. While Castro's political intransigence appears sometimes to be gambling with European support, Europe continues to push for change by offering carrots rather than brandishing sticks.

## CUBA'S CITIES AND TOWNS
### Havana
The image is one of faded glamour, where ancient Chevrolets and Buicks cruise the potholed streets, colonial façades propped up by wooden

 scaffolding peel and crumble from perennial neglect, and plumbing fluctuates from the inadequate to the nonexistent. Yet Havana contains some of the Americas' finest Spanish colonial architecture, and was once a byword for sophistication and elegance. Designated a UNESCO World Heritage Site in 1982, it has benefited from good restoration, still ongoing, and many of the old buildings are now museums.

Havana began life in 1514 as Villa de San Cristóbal de La Habana, on the swampy south side of the island, and moved to its present site in 1519. It replaced Santiago de Cuba as capital in 1553. Its massive fortifications were built in the sixteenth and seventeenth centuries. In the late eighteenth and early nineteenth centuries the city was redesigned along neoclassical lines. Old Havana became a backwater. In the twentieth century fashionable suburbs sprang up, and some historic buildings were replaced by new hotels.

Today Havana is a sprawling city of fifteen municipalities with a population of 2.2 million. Many street names have changed since 1959 but—be alert!—are often still known by their prerevolutionary names.

### Santiago de Cuba

Cuba's second-largest city, with a population of 443,000, is in the far east of the island. Founded in 1515 by Diego Velazquez, it was fortified in the seventeenth century and later became a major slave-trade port. After the Haitian slave revolts of the 1790s, over 25,000 French settlers migrated to Santiago, and their  influence is still evident in its culture. The city saw heavy fighting during the wars of independence, including the U.S. victory over the Spanish fleet in August 1898 that ended them. It was from here that Castro launched his ill-fated assault on the Moncada barracks in 1953, and it suffered greatly from repression by Batista's forces.

Its checkered history has made Santiago a vibrant meltingpot of cultures and architectural styles; but it is best known internationally for music, which today pours from every doorway, day and night. Santiago is the home of *son*, the distinctive Afro-Cuban musical style.

**Camagüey**
Known as Puerto Príncipe until 1903, Camagüey has been the birthplace of generations of revolutionaries since the Ten Years' War. It has many well-preserved colonial buildings, although it lacks the charm of Havana and Santiago.

**Trinidad**
Nestling under the Escambray Mountains, Trinidad has the reputation of being Cuba's

most "unspoiled" town. UNESCO placed it on the World Heritage list in 1988, which may explain the impression it gives of being preserved in aspic, with its pretty pastel-colored houses and narrow cobbled streets made of the very stones used as ballast in the slave and sugar ships.

## Santa Clara

Founded in 1689, this is a pleasant, lively university town—though you could be put off initially by its huge domestic appliance factory, INPUD. Most visitors come to Santa Clara to see Che Guevara's mausoleum.

## Matanzas

Founded in 1683, its name, meaning "massacres," may commemorate the killing of Spaniards by rebellious Indians. In the nineteenth century it was an important center for musicians and writers, and was the birthplace of the *rumba*.

## Guantánamo

This town's name is famous for two things: Joseíto Fernández's song *Guantanamera*, and the U.S. naval base, always a thorn in Cuba's side and notorious since 2002 because of its use to house Afghan detainees.

## Baracoa

This town is Cuba's oldest settlement, and was also the first capital, from 1511 to 1514.

# chapter two

# VALUES & ATTITUDES

What is it about the Cubans that has enabled Cuban socialism to survive for nearly half a century, against considerable odds, while most other socialist experiments have foundered? Clearly it is not simple coercion: the people who saw off the slave-owners, the Spanish, and Batista could have seen off the Castro regime too, but they have not done so. Nor is it the lack of alternative models of development: neoliberal capitalism has long been waiting in the wings, but the current cautious overtures toward capitalism hardly look like a stampede into the arms of big business. Some people say that Cuban society has been held together by the personality of Fidel, but for others that is too big a claim.

This chapter will try to identify some characteristics of the Cuban people that could explain why their society, with all its difficulties, remains so vigorous and vibrant, and some of the contradictions that make Cuba, as the writer Damián J. Fernández put it, "an elusive nation caught between ideals and deep dissatisfaction."

## THE SPIRIT OF THE REVOLUTION
### Patriotism

"*¡Cuba, qué linda es Cuba!*"—"Cuba, how beautiful Cuba is!"—says Cuba's unofficial national anthem, and the verse sums up the Cubans' deeply felt patriotism. Cubans are devoted to their country, and most can't see why anyone would want to live anywhere else— though of course many of them do live somewhere else, in American "Little Havanas" where they do their best to recreate the look, the taste, and the sounds of Cuba itself. Nationalism runs deeper than loyalty to socialism,

and is an enduring feature of *cubanía*, the Cuban spirit, defined by the scholar Fernando Ortiz (1880–1969) as the consciousness of being Cuban and the will and desire to be Cuban that goes beyond mere ownership of a Cuban passport or birth certificate. This is why Martí strikes so strong a chord with Cubans everywhere.

There is also great pride in the achievements of the Revolution. Even critics of the government do not want to lose any of its social and cultural advances. Younger people cannot imagine life without free education and health care, so they complain about other things such as political rigidities and the absence of consumer goods. They tend to be the group most cynical about the government. An ability to condemn individuals but not institutions, and vice versa, is common: people will often say they support Castro but not the Party and "the bureaucracy," or that they hate priests but not the Church.

The hardships of the Special Period have evoked complicated emotional responses in people to life in their country. Many Cubans in all walks of life are utterly committed to the socialist regime and the kind of society it has produced. They feel that what they lack in terms of material possessions is made up for by their cultural wealth, and endure considerable hardship at home rather than seek prosperity abroad, even taking a puritanical view of livelihoods on the margins of legality or the use of private instead of government services. On the other hand, there are obsessive dissenters—and every shade in between. The one thing you will find is that everyone sticks passionately to their point of view. In this highly politicized society, no one is neutral.

**Heroes and Symbols**
Martí is a powerful symbol of the *patria* for Cubans, and both the government and the exile community have made use of this: the exiles by setting up Radio Martí to beam anti-Castro

propaganda at Cuba, and the government by
tactically downplaying socialism and invoking
Martí to appeal to nationalist sentiments. Castro
is still idolized by many, especially the aging but
still numerous generation of those he liberated.
Some sources, however, hint that there are
people who hate Fidel in private but profess to
love him in public, out of fear—a
suggestion practically impossible
to confirm or deny.

The hero whose name is
constantly invoked, not just in
official rhetoric but in everyday
discourse, is Che Guevara. The
constant coda to criticism of
Fidel is "We need another Che."

**Community and Cooperation**
The Cubans' sense of community, already strong
before the Revolution, has been nurtured since
1959 not only by the creation of neighborhood
committees and mass organizations, but by the
sharing of dramatic experiences of both
prosperity and adversity. In particular, the sudden
sharp downturn in living standards after 1989,
which affected everybody, united citizens rather
than producing the predicted collapse of society.
Many foreigners are impressed by this community
spirit and by the ease with which Cubans value

collective interests often over their own individual interests. The neighborhood is important, and people cooperate naturally, helping and looking out for each other.

Cubans treat each other—and visitors—with courtesy but not deference. The revolutionary form of address, *Compañero* (Comrade) is still widely used. Cubans may seek money and material comfort, but on the whole they do not seek social status, and are unpretentious. The gap between the highest and lowest earners is still relatively small, though it is now widening.

Given the shocking levels of inequality in pre-1959 Cuban society, this egalitarianism and cooperative spirit does seem at least partly attributable to the Revolution's determination to erase inequalities of class, race, and gender.

**DISSENT**

Paradoxically for such a nation of patriots, Cubans are also quick to vote with their feet. The tendency of serious anti-Castroists to leave the country rather than stay at home and organize an internal opposition may also help to explain the regime's longevity. Internal opposition is not very organized and is therefore weak and ineffectual. Though you may hear plenty of complaints from people you meet in Cuba, it is actually very difficult to get hard, objective evidence of the "opposition movement," not only because it naturally excites extreme passions in Cubans on either side but because the Cuban penchant for both secrecy and exaggeration often gets in the way of the truth. Some writers have noticed a high capacity for duplicity among Cubans: nobody is quite who they seem to be, large numbers of people are allegedly connected to the security services in some way, and as a visitor you'll be very unlikely to find out who or how.

## Bitching About Bureaucracy

The kind of dissent that gets people arrested is not the same thing, however, as grumbling about the government and particularly bureaucracy, which has been a national sport ever since the 1960s. Cubans tend to blame obtuse, rule-bound bureaucrats for every problem that can't be attributed to the U.S. embargo. At the same time they can be infuriatingly bureaucratic themselves, once installed behind a desk, as anyone who has hung around Havana airport waiting for a nonstandard visa to be stamped can attest.

Fidel himself made complaining about the bureaucracy legitimate when he declared in a speech to the National Assembly in 1993 that the civil service "must be streamlined." The absurdities of bureaucracy have been the subject of comic critique in Cuban films such as *Death of a Bureaucrat* (1966) and *Guantanamera* (1995).

In fact Cubans are always kicking in small ways against their nanny state, finding ways around rules or simply ignoring them. The legions of people who offer services to tourists that are strictly speaking illegal is a very visible example; but a broad streak of anarchism goes back at least to the early workers' movement and the influence of anarcho-syndicalist Spanish immigrants in the first years of the twentieth century, and has helped to temper the Cuban brand of socialism.


## MULTIRACIAL CUBA

Cuba is a true meltingpot of races, the descendants of Spanish conquerors and later migrants, French exiles, African slaves, Chinese indentured laborers, and others, including some indigenous Taínos. Intermarriage has been common for centuries, and up to 70 percent of the population is estimated to be of mixed race. Cuban culture owes a tremendous amount to this kaleidoscopic heritage.

Declaring racial equality was one of the first acts of the Revolution and legislation to abolish discrimination was quickly passed. Older black Cubans who experienced this still praise Fidel for it. But, though officially racial discrimination no longer exists, in practice it is all too alive. The revolution gave black Cubans health care, education, and decent employment, but—despite the departure of many rich whites—light-skinned Cubans continued to run the show. Indeed nearly all the revolutionary leaders were white. Even now not many black Cubans have top jobs, though there are some rising political stars and many black professionals. There is some evidence that black Cubans are acquiring fewer jobs than whites in the well-paid tourist sector. Young black men (both Cubans and foreigners!) are stopped by the police more often than anyone else.

Until recently, discussing race in Cuban society was taboo, and the antiracist legislation meant that while there could be no whites-only clubs or meeting places, there could be no blacks-only ones either, making it hard for black people to discuss racism together. There are still some fears that raising the race question may threaten the national unity the government feels is essential to face down the US.A. Since around 1998, however, Cuban academics and government officials have begun trying to understand why racial discrimination and stereotyping are so hard to eradicate from this avowedly egalitarian society. Castro's presence at the UN World Conference on Racism (Durban, 2001) may have given a push in the right direction. Conferences and exhibitions addressing the issue are held, and young black people are using rap music to denounce racism and demand to be treated as equals.

## ATTITUDES TOWARD RELIGION

Catholicism survived quietly throughout the period of Communist repression; but Cuba was never as Catholic a country as others in Latin America, and in particular Catholicism made scant inroads into the black population because of the strength of Afro-Cuban religion. Although the Cuban Constitution states: "The State recognizes, respects and guarantees religious freedom," in reality, the Church hardly existed for almost four decades. Soon after 1959 it became a focus of opposition to Castro's regime, which retaliated by closing Church schools and many churches and slashing the numbers of the priesthood. Protestant churches and even synagogues came under the same prohibitions.

However, since the Church was officially re-recognized in 1998, the numbers of Cubans interested in Christian religious practice and values has been growing. People who had abandoned or hidden their Catholicism are returning to the Church. Protestant congregations, including Baptists, Methodists,

Quakers, and Pentecostals, survived better, though Jehovah's Witnesses were banned outright in 1975. Judaism was also severely restricted for many years—most of Cuba's 15,000 Jews fled when Castro took power—but is now reemerging. There are synagogues in Havana and Camagüey. The Muslim community is several thousand strong, mostly of Lebanese descent.

Unfortunately, there are already reports that the revived Catholic Church in Cuba may be losing touch with social concerns and the needs of the poor, and also that the security forces are continuing to monitor church services. Whatever the truth of these, it seems that the Church is prepared to play a political role. In September 2003, the Cuban bishops chose the feast day of the nationally revered Virgin of El Cobre, historically related to struggles for freedom, to issue a pastoral letter criticizing current government policies.

**Afro-Cuban Religion**
The religion of the Yoruba people came to Cuba in the slave ships and evolved over the centuries into the Afro-Cuban religion generally known as *santería*. For a long time it was limited to peasant communities, but it is now found everywhere and is practiced by Cubans of every color,

age, political persuasion, and walk of life, from
rural farmers to government ministers. For a great
many people it is a powerful guide to life. Afro-
Cuban culture is to a great extent defined by
religion, posing a potential contradiction to the
Revolution's commitment to secularism.

Afro-Cuban religion began to have a higher
profile internationally when the government
realized it was culturally interesting to foreigners.
Abakuá dances, for instance, started to feature in
the repertoire of the national folklore dance
company, foreign visitors would be invited to
witness *santería* ceremonies, and books on Afro-
Cuban lore and religion began to fill the shelves in
bookshops. The movement is growing to rescue
Afro-Cuban religion from folklore, disentangle it
from Christian syncretisms, and recover its
original values and traditional practices.

**MEN AND WOMEN**

An image of Cuba prevalent among tourists,
particularly men, is that it is a permissive place,
where sex is always on the agenda and women are
bold and willing. It is true that Cubans talk volubly
and frankly about sex, as about most things; but
these attitudes are highly colored by a pervasive
*machismo*. At the same time, sexual life is
conditioned by the Revolution's genuine desire to

promote equality between men and women. Thus the divorce rate is high, consensual unions are common, and the availability of abortion lightens the pressure on people to avoid pre- or extramarital sex. Cuban women are more independent than in many other developing countries: they have jobs and incomes and the state provides child care, so they are not economically chained to unsatisfactory relationships. Yet family life is very important to Cubans. The culture idealizes motherhood and children, and most young women want to find a husband and have a family. Women who become prostitutes usually do so for harsh economic reasons.

Cuban *machismo* has been called the worst in Latin America. Its historical roots lie in the relatively recent abolition of slavery, in which women were owned as property and slave owners had sexual rights over them. A masculine culture of multiple partners and domestic violence persists, despite legislation and policies for equality such as the Family Code of 1975 and more recent attention to rising domestic violence caused by the economic crisis.

Although the national organization for women (*Federación de Mujeres Cubanas*, or FMC) has been very active in the promotion of education and equal employment for women, its concerns are largely determined by Party priorities. It has condemned the return of prostitution, but, disappointingly, without recognizing the economic factors that have driven women into it.

Despite a softening in official attitudes to homosexuality, there is still a lot of thoughtless and ill-informed prejudice against lesbians and gay men, particularly among heterosexual men.

## ATTITUDES TOWARD FOREIGNERS

Cubans are unfailingly welcoming to foreign visitors—surprisingly, perhaps, given the way tourism has once again limited their access to places where the well-off play—and treat them with intense curiosity and interest. For many years Cubans were well acquainted with nations and people about whom the Western world knew little—Russians, Bulgarians, Czechs, Yugoslavs, East Germans. But, although the Soviet Union was Cuba's economic savior for three decades, the Cubans were never particularly fond of Eastern Europeans—particularly Russians—or their culture, and they were often treated privately as figures of fun. At the same time, they felt cut off from Western Europe and tended to quiz visitors mercilessly about it. They still do.

Much greater cultural affinity is expressed with both Latin America and the United States.

Attitudes to Latin Americans vary according to country and tend to be colored by a country's politics; Mexico in particular is seen as a bastion of solidarity. But there is a general view among Cubans that in terms of education, health, and social welfare they are much better off than people in other countries, and have a slight sense of superiority for that reason.

Culturally, Cuba's recognition of the links with other Caribbean countries is strong. To many black and mixed-race Cubans, Africa represents an ancestral homeland, and the growth of Afro-Cuban studies reflects this heritage.

Not surprisingly, Cuban views of the U.S.A. are complex. While political opposition is one of the things that unite Cuban citizens, opinions of the U.S. people are more nuanced and sensitive. Cubans responded to Hurricane Katrina in 2005 by expressing solidarity with the poor—and especially the black—population of the affected areas. Practically everyone in Cuba has relatives or friends living in the United States, and Cuban culture is very American, a legacy of the years of American colonization, which is when much of the current urban infrastructure was built. The passion for baseball (*beisbol*) and the persistence of American nicknames for things, such as *chevy* for a taxi, hint at this cultural affinity. Cubans are fascinated by American consumer goods.

## HUMOR

While it's probably not true that, as one commentator says, Cubans refuse to take life seriously, they do tend to respond to hard times and political restrictions with sardonic, irreverent humor. *Choteo* (joking, or mockery) in Cuba refers to a quite long tradition of political satire, which serves as both commentary and safety valve. Big political events such as the Pope's visit in 1998 tend to set off a fusillade of jokes that ricochets around the country. Opinions differ as to whether you can safely make jokes (apart from affectionate ones) about national leaders, but you can certainly make them about bureaucracy, transportation, the economic crisis, the availability and quality of food, and so on. Cubans like verbal jokes and puns, and giving things and people bizarre nicknames. There are excellent political cartoonists, largely employed in U.S. bashing. As a visitor, however, you would be very unwise to make jokes about national leaders or the ideological basis of the Revolution.

## MAKING THE BEST OF IT

Finally, Cubans have been immensely inventive and resilient throughout their history. They are experts at making do and mending—a quality that brought them through the austerities of the Special

Period with flying colors. The classic example of this is the way antique American cars have been preserved for half a century, in the absence of spare parts, and are still being used; but this inventiveness can also be seen in the experiments in ecological conservation, recycling, and especially organic agriculture, in which the Special Period was neatly turned to advantage. It may not be too fanciful to see in the restless, inventive Cuban

spirit a factor in the development of Cuban socialism and its pragmatic refusal simply to copy the Stalinist model.

Cubans also possess the spirit of enterprise. Even during the 1980s little businesses would spring up at the slightest opportunity, even if they were closed down a couple of weeks later. The legalization of self-employment in 1993 caused an immediate rush of small business registrations; some of these micro-businesses almost certainly already existed clandestinely.

Cubans' unquenchable sense of community, generosity of spirit, sharp and critical humor, even their readiness to complain and circumvent petty rules, are evidence of a resilient, resourceful people full of hope and determination.

# CUSTOMS & TRADITIONS

Africans, Europeans, and people of mixed descent have lived side by side, though not on equal terms, in Cuba for nearly five centuries. Cuban culture is thus a complex blend of African and European—chiefly Spanish—traits. In 1975 Fidel Castro declared the country to be "Afro-Latin," and it is increasingly recognized that Afro-Cuban culture and religion are central to its identity.

Grafted on to this heritage is the official culture of the Revolution, which, though highly institutionalized, has coalesced into a set of cultural practices and landmarks that form a permanent background to people's lives.

## CATHOLIC TRADITIONS

Cuba inherited the Spanish Catholic calendar, full of dramatic and colorful ceremonies. Manifestations of the Virgin Mary were particularly popular. Some traditions persisted after the Revolution despite the suppression of the

Church, especially that of the Virgin of Charity of El Cobre, Cuba's patron Saint.

### LA VIRGEN DE LA CARIDAD DEL COBRE

The story goes that in 1606 three men were miraculously saved from a storm at sea when a board bearing a wooden statue of the Virgin of Charity appeared floating on the waves. The statue was taken to the mine at El Cobre, near Santiago de Cuba, where a shrine was built for it and, in 1927, a large church. In 1916 the Virgin of Charity of El Cobre officially became Cuba's patron saint. Her worship never dimmed, even during the high revolutionary period, and she has long been linked with struggles for freedom; thus she appeals equally to supporters of the Revolution in Cuba and their opponents in exile. In *santería* she is equated with Oshún, the goddess of love, wealth, and fresh water, and one of the most popular *orishas*, or gods.

On the feast day of the Virgin pilgrims flock to El Cobre from all over the island as the statue of the Virgin is carried in procession through the streets.

Many religious traditions are reemerging now that the Church can operate openly once more. Christmas Day has been restored as a public holiday, but not Good Friday, Easter, Epiphany, and other key moments in the Christian year, which are celebrated only in churches. Other traditions being revived include the old Spanish Maytime Pilgrimage of the Cross (*Romerías de la Cruz de Mayo*), preserved in Holguín, where devotees climb 450 steps leading up to a cross overlooking the city. Many saints' days, particularly those of local patron saints, are marked with masses and street celebrations. Havana celebrates the feast of its patron saint, St. Christopher, with a solemn mass in the cathedral.

## AFRO-CUBAN TRADITIONS

The African religions that put down roots in Cuba—chiefly that of the Yoruba slaves and their descendants—were shaped by the need to escape persecution. The people disguised the identities of their gods, the *orishas*, under the names of Catholic saints: thus Elegguá, the first god to be invoked during ceremonies, was concealed behind the Holy Child of Atocha; Obatalá, the great *orisha* and maker of human beings, is associated with the Immaculate Conception or the Virgin of Mercy; Yemayá, goddess of the sea, with the Virgin of

Regla, the patron saint of the port of Havana; Shangó, the god of thunder and war but also of music and dance, with Saint Barbara, and so on. The Yorubas' supreme deity has three aspects, Olodumare, Olofi, and Olorún, which invited association with the Christian Trinity. The resulting fusion became known in Spanish as *santería*. In reality, however, the devotees were worshiping their own pantheon, which contains as many as four hundred regional or tribal *orishas*. The true African name for *santería* translates as the Rule of Oshá.

Whole books have been written on the practice of *santería*. The priests, called *babalawos*, undergo rigorous initiation and training. Rituals are performed in the home—a legacy of the history of concealment—where decorated altars are set up. Music and dance are central, with songs for each *orisha*, and dances reflecting their qualities. During a ceremony a celebrant may be possessed by the god invoked. The sacrifice of small animals is an integral part of the ceremonies.

Other Afro-Cuban cults are the *palo monte* (the Rule of Mayombé), introduced to Cuba by Congolese and Angolan slaves and based on the cult of the dead; and *Abakuá*, not strictly speaking a religion but a secret society open only to men, which became dominated by whites and earned a sinister reputation for violence under Batista. Today, Abakuá is closer to a kind of Afro-Cuban freemasonry. The masked and hooded *diablito* (little devil), a figure from Abakuá ceremonies, has become part of Cuban folklore.

## CELEBRATING HISTORY

Cuba shares with other socialist societies an enthusiasm for political and historical anniversaries and for naming days and years. Every year since 1959 has been given a name, for example, "Year of the Agrarian Reform" (1960), "Year of the Heroic Guerrilla" (1968, the year after Che's death), "Year of Institutionalization" (1977), "Year of the 30th Anniversary of the *Granma* Landing" (1986). The difficulty of maintaining this pattern is illustrated by 2005's title, "Year of the Bolivarian Alternative for the Americas."

Similarly, the calendar bristles with revolutionary feast days marked with speeches and rallies. They commemorate events such as the birthday of José Martí (January 28), the 1895 War of Independence (February 24), the Bay of Pigs incident (April 19), the deaths of Che Guevara (October 6), Camilo Cienfuegos (October 28), and the Martyrs of the Revolution (June 30), and key battles in the independence wars and the revolutionary struggle. There are days in honor of women (International Women's Day, March 8), children (April 4), teachers (December 22), and others.

## CULTURAL EVENTS

As part of its promotion of culture and of the nation, the government sponsors dozens of festivals devoted to film, music, and dance of all kinds, literature, books, Afro-Cuban culture, and so on. Some are annual, some biennial; some are international in scope, such as the international book or film festivals (see page 117), some extremely local, such as the festival of the cockerel in the town of Morón or the grapefruit harvest festival at Nueva Gerona on the Isle of Youth. Specialist festivals, such as the festival of steam, based in old sugar mills and factories, draw international enthusiasts. Cuba also hosts national and international conferences throughout the year, often on medical or scientific subjects.

## SOME CULTURAL FESTIVALS

**April:** *PERCUBA*, international percussion and drum festival, Havana.
**May:** *Festival de Baile*, dance, Santiago de Cuba. May Festival, traditional music and dance, Holguín.

**June:** *Festival Boleros de Oro*, concerts by Cuban and international performers of *bolero* songs, Havana, Santiago, and Morón.

**June, biennially:** *Jornada Cucalambeana, Encuentro Iberoamericano de la Décima*, Cuban country music and poetry, Las Tunas.

**August:** *Cubadanza*, contemporary dance, Havana. *Festival de Rap Cubana Habana Hip Hop*, Alamar.

**August, biennially:** *Festival Internacional de Música Popular "Beny Moré,"* honoring this popular musician, Cienfuegos, Lajas, and Havana.

**September, biennially:** *Matamoros Son*, festival of *son* music.

**November:** *Festival de Raíces Africanas Wemilere*, government-sponsored Afro-Cuban festival, Guanabacoa.

**December:** *Fiesta a la Guantanamera*, Afro-Cuban and French-Haitian music, culture, and folklore, Guantánamo.

## PUBLIC HOLIDAYS

Until Christmas Day was reinstated as an official public holiday in 1997, all Cuba's public holidays commemorated political and historical events, chiefly with speeches, rallies, and gatherings in towns and cities. There are just five official public holidays when offices and shops close (although most restaurants and tourist facilities function as normal). New Year's Day is celebrated countrywide, because it coincides with the anniversary of the day of liberation and the end of the Batista dictatorship. International Labor Day brings out the most participants, and rallies and marches are held everywhere. In Havana thousands of banner-waving students and mass organization members march past Fidel in front of the Martí monument in Havana's Plaza de la Revolución, but the crowds that once topped a million have dwindled in recent years. Similar events on a smaller scale mark July 26, the anniversary of the assault on the Moncada barracks, and October 10, the anniversary of the start of the Ten Years' War, the first major struggle for Cuban independence.

Public transportation is more unreliable than ever on public holidays, but on May 1 cavalcades of buses shuttle people to the mass rallies in every city and town.

| January 1 | Anniversary of the Triumph of the Revolution/ New Year's Day |
|-----------|---------------------------------------------------------------|
| May 1 | International Labor Day |
| July 26 | Commemoration of the National Rebellion |
| October 10 | *Día del Grito de Yara* |
| December 25 | Christmas Day |

## CARNIVALS

Cuban *Carnaval* (Carnival),
like so much of Cuban
popular culture, has its roots
in the slave era and the rare
moments when slaves were
allowed to sing and dance. In
the nineteenth century the end of

the sugar harvest was celebrated with processions
in which dancing troupes known as *comparsas*
would compete. This developed into the present
Carnaval at the turn of the twentieth century,
with competing teams dancing through the streets
in masks and colorful costumes and carrying
banners and paper lanterns.

Before 1959 private companies sponsored
*comparsas* from different neighborhoods, but after
that, instead of consumer goods, they found
themselves advertising revolutionary policies.
During the Special Period most annual
celebrations were suspended, but Carnaval is now
regaining its former glory. Carnaval bands use
several kinds of drum, including the *tumba
francesa*, brought from Haiti by the slaves of
exiled French planters, and the *corneta china*, the
Chinese cornet or trumpet, a late-nineteenth-
century introduction. Looming over the parades
are large gaudy floats carrying giant papier mâché
animals or human caricatures.

Havana has two carnivals a year, one in February and the main one in July and August, when top bands play nightly to dense crowds along the Malecón, the city's broad seafront promenade, and elsewhere around the city. The highlight, on the final weekend, is a spectacular parade of floats that winds its way from Old Havana down the Malecón. Santiago de Cuba hosts Cuba's most lavish carnival in June, with splendidly costumed parades and floats, all-night music, and parties. The entire city is illuminated and all doors are decorated. Camagüey has a smaller but still exciting and colorful version, also in June, and there are other carnivals at Pinar del Río (June), Ciego de Ávila (March, rather tourist oriented), and Varadero (late January to early February, unalloyed tourism).

Finally, a highly popular carnival-like event lasting for much of Advent is the Parrandas de Remedios, held in Remedios and neighboring villages, December 8–24. Originating in 1829, when the parish priest of Remedios got the village children to bang on sheets of tin to wake up the inhabitants for Advent masses, the festival begins with a children's parade and culminates in a

contest between two quarters of the town, San
Salvador and Carmen, to make the most noise.
The *fiesta* ends with fireworks on Christmas
Eve—but never before 3:00 a.m.

## SOME RITES OF PASSAGE

Economic crisis has not dampened Cubans'
enthusiasm for weddings—ends can always be
made to meet for the celebration. The
revolutionary government established an
institution for secular weddings, the Palacio de los
Matrimonios, opening the first "palace" in a
former gambling hall in Havana in 1966. The
wedding ceremony at a *palacio* takes only fifteen
minutes, and successive wedding groups cross on
the *palacio's* broad stairs. The simplest celebration
is cheap, with a rented wedding dress and modest
allocations of food, beer, and rum available on the
ration, but as the Special Period slackened
families have begun to splurge out on more
luxurious celebrations, with expensive dresses,
caterers, and cars.

For girls in all Latin American countries, the
fifteenth birthday (*los quince*) is a special event,
signifying the young girl's entry into womanhood.
Cuba is no exception. Typically, the birthday girl (*la
quinceañera*) is fêted with a banquet, complete with
big cake, at which she dances formally with her

father and male relatives, and then with her boyfriend or a male friend. Fifteenth-birthday celebrations—often very ostentatious ones—were popular in Cuba until the Revolution, but then became lower-key. However, families still dig deep into their pockets to give their daughters a special event. Photographs and videos of the *quinceañera* in a variety of costumes are usually taken. In recent years expensive *quinces* have made a comeback, often with financial help from well-off relatives abroad, and the celebratory mass is being held again. Weddings, baptisms, and funerals are also increasingly being celebrated in church since 1998.

# THE CUBANS AT HOME

**QUALITY OF LIFE**

Cuba has never been a rich country, and now it is unequivocally poor in material resources. Nonetheless, in 2004 it ranked fifty-second in the world and seventh in Latin America and the Caribbean, according to the UN's Human Development Index, which uses criteria such as life expectancy, school enrollment, and literacy, as well as income, to measure a country's development. Living in Cuba can seem like inhabiting a time warp, with its sit-up-and-beg bicycles, its shabby, romantic architecture, its much-mended machinery, and its lack of competitive killer instinct (though there is no lack of entrepreneurial energy); but to many who have experienced the country, its true riches are its people and its collective spirit.

Most Cubans struggle daily to make ends meet. The word they use is *resolver*, to solve or resolve, a revealing word that suggests that making ends meet is a problem to be solved, not an insuperable crisis. Personal prosperity depends heavily on what currency you hold. People working in tourism consider themselves lucky since they have easy access to foreign currency or convertible pesos. State salaries paid in ordinary Cuban pesos are very low indeed, so even highly qualified professionals have other sources of income, licit and otherwise.

In mid-2005 the average wage was around 200 pesos per month, equivalent to 8 CUC at the standard rate of 25:1. Professionals earned 300 to 500 pesos a month. Some state enterprises related to tourism and others with sound earnings in hard currencies periodically give bonuses to dedicated and punctual workers—a contrast to the system of "socialist emulation," where the incentives for commitment and good work are moral, not material. "Mixed enterprises" (see pages 43 and 143) are supposed to pay only in pesos, but regularly give a premium in CUC to their employees, according to their rank.

On the other hand, many of the things on which people in other countries spend much of their earnings are free or very cheap to Cubans.
Many people now own their own homes, and repayments on government mortgages are set at a

maximum of 10 percent of the chief breadwinner's income, which is also the rate at which rent is set. Education is free at all levels, and so is health care. Gas, electricity, and telephone services are all subsidized by the state.

## TOWN AND COUNTRY

The Revolution changed rural life much more than urban. Fidel's experiences in the remote, impoverished Sierra Maestra confirmed his commitment to improving the lives of peasants, producers of the country's main sources of wealth. The agrarian reform of 1960 gave land to the poorest rural people, sharecroppers and landless peasants, first in cooperatives, then in state farms, while small farmers were organized into the National Association of Small Farmers (ANAP). Since 1993, almost all state-owned agricultural land has been turned over to cooperatives, paid according to production.

Whatever the faults of collectivization, it did enable the government to improve the living conditions of peasants. A policy of "rural urbanization" narrowed the gap between town and country living standards by providing electricity, running water, education, and health care facilities to villages. Hundreds of new rural settlements were built: today multistory apartment blocks can be seen in the middle of the countryside, towering over tobacco or cane fields. Conversely, the Special Period provided the impetus for some "urban ruralization." Vacant lots and city parks were used for intensive organic horticulture and town dwellers were encouraged to use their gardens to grow food.

## HOUSING

The urban reform that accompanied the land reform in 1960 slashed rents and redirected rent revenues to the state instead of the landlords. Many homes of the rich were simply taken over by their servants when the owners fled. Most of these homes have become the property of their inhabitants. New homes can be bought from the state at a low-interest mortgage. In the 1960s and '70s, many apartment blocks were built by volunteer labor, the builders gaining the right to  an apartment in the completed building.

However, dwellings can be very overcrowded, particularly in Havana's old central *barrios*, where there is simply no room to expand. The right of tenure is inalienable, and private houses are passed on only by inheritance, so there is no housing market and families just stay put even if they grow, unless they can arrange an exchange. Cuba has a long tradition of extended families living together, but overcrowding can lead to frayed nerves and family quarrels.

Most of the country is electrified, but the service is sporadic and unpredictable, and timetables for when water and electricity are available are unreliable. In remote parts of the country solar panels are being introduced. Power outages (cuts) are the subject of many wry jokes; and it has been noticed that tourist resorts and hotels, the generators of national income, are often blazing with light when the rest of the country is in darkness.

## HEALTH CARE

The health care system is generally agreed to be one of the Cuban Revolution's greatest achievements and to have raised Cubans' health indices to industrialized country levels. All Cubans get free health care by right. The Revolution's first priorities were ensuring universal access to health care and eradicating the main infectious diseases by mass vaccination campaigns. The Family Doctor service was established in the 1980s to relieve the pressure on clinics and hospitals and to serve remote rural areas, each family doctor looking after roughly 120 families. Young doctors doing their rounds on horseback became a familiar sight among the mountain villages.

However, the health system has suffered from a severe shortage of resources because of the U.S. embargo and the loss of Eastern European support. There is no shortage of trained personnel—indeed, Cuba sends doctors to other countries as a gesture of solidarity—or of health infrastructure, but a dire shortage of medicines. The government has therefore made a priority of preventive health care and is increasingly exploring the use of natural medicine, with a program of medicinal herb cultivation incorporated into organic agriculture. Meanwhile, more people are resorting to folk medicine as practiced by devotees of *santería*.

As food shortages worsened during the early 1990s, international health organizations were predicting the return of nutrition-related diseases to Cuba, but the most serious results of this were averted by prioritizing protection of the most vulnerable people, children under five, and newborns and their mothers. Other diseases, such as typhoid fever and tuberculosis, also reemerged because water could not be purified in some areas. On the other hand, the Special Period had unintended positive effects on people's health, as they began to eat more vegetables and fruit and to take more exercise by walking and cycling. The absence of chemical inputs and automobile fumes has also improved food, soil, and air quality.

Hospitals have also become shabby and under-equipped during the Special Period, and their way of making ends meet has unfortunately once again created a division between haves and have-nots, since the government has begun to take on paying patients from abroad to subsidize the state hospitals.

**HIV/AIDS in Cuba**

According to UNAIDS, Cuba was one of the first countries to take AIDS seriously and devise a response combining prevention and care. However, the nature of that response is highly controversial. All Cuban AIDS patients are segregated in special sanatoriums, and HIV testing (using Cuban-produced kits) has become very general through a national screening program.

Draconian as this policy may seem, its results are incontrovertible. At 0.05 percent in 2003, Cuba's HIV infection rate is one of the lowest in the world. According to a foreign writer who visited one in 2002, the sanatoriums are pleasant, comfortable places where patients benefit from care and can have weekend passes and family visits. It is notable, too, that AIDS patients continue to receive their wages while they are in a sanatorium.

The U.S. embargo deprived Cuba of antiretroviral drugs until 2001, when Cuban laboratories began manufacturing generic versions. Now Cuba is one of the few developing countries to offer all of its people with HIV/AIDS an adequate supply of medication.

**Disability**
The approach to disability is not as enlightened as the general approach to health care. Disabled people are guaranteed adequate health, rehabilitation, and employment services, but they are cared for in institutions rather than in the community, and employed in special factories. This approach is paternalistic but is perhaps the only affordable alternative to making the whole country disability-friendly. Disabled visitors will find few places accessible to wheelchairs or otherwise adapted for disabled people.

Mental health has also been addressed. Before 1959 there was only one public psychiatric hospital in Cuba. There are now three, in Havana, Camagüey, and Santiago de Cuba, and psychiatric units are attached to some general hospitals.

## EDUCATION

Cuba's achievements in education are woı
renowned. Education is free at all levels
from preschool day care to university and
lifelong learning, resulting in a well-
educated and generally well-read
workforce. Following the thinking of
both Marx and Martí, the education
system combines schooling with practical
experience in various ways, including taking city
children to the countryside for six weeks a year.
There are also semi-boarding schools in the
countryside where students combine classes with
agricultural tasks during the week and go home
on weekends. Critics of the Revolution see these
simply as strategies for extracting cheap labor
from young people, but they could equally be seen
as ways of inculcating from an early age
community spirit, consideration for others, and
understanding of how the economy works.

### The Battle of Ideas

As so often, these big achievements are now under
threat for lack of resources—but they are also seen
as being in danger of being undermined by
capitalist values. The Battle of Ideas, now in its fifth
year, is a large educational campaign spanning well
over a hundred projects and intended to counteract
some of the negative social effects of tourism, such

as a drop in the number of young people wanting to become teachers. In an emergency program aiming to get class sizes down to twenty, over 5,500 young people were trained as primary schoolteachers and then worked in their local primary school while continuing their own higher studies. Other projects include training courses for social workers, the launch of an educational television channel, increased provision of TVs, VCRs, and computers in schools, and a TV program for distance learning known as University for All.

## THE CHANGING FAMILY
The Revolution has changed the way Cuban families live. Historically, extended families of three generations lived together, but this is less common nowadays because of housing pressures, especially in Havana, as well as short-lived marriages. Many Cubans have been through three marriages by the age of forty. People are having fewer children, and the number of households headed by women is increasing, partly because most emigrants since 1980 are men.

The population is also aging, and the country has one of the highest proportions of senior citizens in Latin America, partly as a result of good health care for the elderly.

The Cuban diaspora has serious impacts on the Cuban family; separation is painful whatever the motive for exile. Sometimes emigration divides families politically, but more often family members on both sides of the Florida Straits strive to preserve family unity, especially when people have emigrated for economic reasons. Many Cuban-Americans were angry in 2003 about President Bush's harsh measures cutting the frequency of permitted family visits to the island to once every three years.

## THE DAILY ROUND

Cubans may seem laid back, but they lead extremely busy lives. The usual urban workday is roughly 8:30 a.m. to 5:30 p.m., Monday to Friday, with a one-hour lunch break; some workplaces also open on Saturday mornings. Many people make long and tedious journeys to work. In the countryside, the day regularly begins before dawn and finishes after dark.

The female members of the household do most of the domestic chores. The 1975 Family Code has had very little impact on the traditional distribution of housework; taking the children to school or fetching the shopping is often the limit of a father's practical involvement in running the home. The austerity regime of the Special Period increased women's domestic labor, too, as more food had to prepared at home rather than bought, transportation between home and work took longer, and families could no longer afford to pay others to do laundry and cleaning.

In the evenings there are classes and cultural and other activities, but there is also time for just hanging out. Cubans visit each other frequently, and not necessarily with advance notice. Almost anything can be an occasion for a party at someone's home. On weekends during the hotter months, streams of buses take people to the beaches outside Havana. A growing number of Cubans now also go to church on Sundays, young people making up much of the congregations.

### La Libreta

Rationing was introduced early in 1962 and has never ceased, though the range and quantities of products available on the ration book (*libreta*) fluctuate. The *libreta* covers staple foods and some shoes and clothes, particularly children's clothes. Newlyweds get a cake, three boxes of beer, and a special clothing ration. These products are bought at general stores called *bodegas*, always distinguishable by the lines outside them. Working families often send elderly members of the household to do the waiting in line for them.

## IN THE COMMUNITY

Cuba's tradition of night classes goes right back to the 1961 literacy campaign, when much of the teaching took place by the light of a storm lantern after the day's work in the fields or the home was over. Now Cubans of all ages take part in a vast array of community-based activities in the evenings, including night classes, music, dance or theater group rehearsals, sports, and meetings.

### Volunteer Work

Volunteer labor (*trabajo voluntario*) was introduced in 1962 as a temporary measure to bring in that year's sugar harvest and was later extended to other economic activities, including construction. It was constitutionally recognized in 1976 as a "forger of the communist conscience of our people." It is one of the clearest expressions of Che Guevara's conviction that moral rather than material incentives were a key principle of the new society. Several special days of mass volunteering were held in 2004 to celebrate the forty-fifth anniversary of the Revolution.

It is debated how truly voluntary *trabajo voluntario* is; although many people certainly do it out of commitment, others may be succumbing to social pressures from the government, the Party, or their workplace management and union branch, or undertaking volunteer work because it may increase their opportunities to get hold of certain scarce consumer items. People are paid their ordinary wage while doing volunteer work, so no one loses money. A pragmatic issue is the risk of using unqualified people in skilled trades such as construction.

**The CDRs**
Membership of the Committees for the Defense of the Revolution is high—in the millions, according to pro-government sources—and, while not strictly speaking obligatory, reportedly necessary if you want to get ahead in the community or the Party. The organization was explicitly created for surveillance (see page 39), and was restructured at the end of the 1980s to respond to the needs of the Special Period. It still carries out crime-watching functions—in 2005 a "national surveillance exercise" was held to mark the forty-fifth anniversary of the organization's foundation—but it is not clear how far this extends to political espionage.

In other areas, such as coordinating disaster response, blood donation, vaccination and other public health campaigns, and recycling, the CDRs perform a vital service; but they have also been responsible for organizing threatening "rapid-response" gatherings outside the houses of dissidents.

# chapter five

# MAKING FRIENDS

Meeting the intensely sociable Cubans couldn't be easier; but managing the relationship can be tricky for a number of reasons. Cubans' relentless ebullience and curiosity—the very things that make it so easy to meet them—can be both startling on first acquaintance and exhausting after a while for reserved Britons and even for many North Americans. It seems churlish to issue this warning when people are so universally kind and friendly, but wise visitors will use discretion and some caution, both political and sexual, in their relationships with Cubans.

## MEETING PEOPLE

The Cuban way of life is very accessible to foreigners, especially to those who speak Spanish. Much of life is lived on the street or in the open doorway, and people are genuinely interested in each other. Even in the crowded center of Havana, it is impossible to feel anonymous, as one does in most large Western cities: people will make eye contact as they pass, and someone will soon begin talking to you. If you ask for directions to a place, you are very likely to be taken there, especially if your Spanish isn't good. "Stranger danger" doesn't seem to be a Cuban concept. This kindness is all the more remarkable since the preferential treatment of foreigners has  recreated to some extent the inequalities the Revolution abolished.

However, if you don't like being asked personal questions, don't go to Cuba. *Everyone* will ask where you come from and will want to know all about you, your family, and your country. It's well-intentioned and understandable, particularly from people who have not themselves traveled, but it is wearing. The wonderful Cuban spirit of neighborhood and community, and the lack of privacy, are two sides of the same coin.

**Hospitality**

Cubans are pathologically hospitable, and are quite likely to invite you home the first time they meet you, insisting that you share their meal or stay the nigh If you want to refuse, it may be hard to know how to do so gracefully! If you do accept such an invitation, however, you should try to find a way to contribute something to the meal, or bring a small g___, and be prepared to reciprocate. If you eat out together, you should bear in mind that the relationship between you and your Cuban friends will be economically unequal, and be prepared to pay for the meal and drinks.

Should you arrive on time at someone's home? It's actually perfectly polite to be a little late—but not too late. Cubans' unpunctuality is legendary, but in fact they tend to be punctual when it matters, and not when it doesn't. Fluid timekeeping in social life is very understandable, especially considering that one can be penalized for arriving even ten minutes late at work, however bad the transportation.

## Joining Clubs and Societies

If you are staying in Cuba for a significant length of time, joining in a local activity such as a choir, dance classes, or a study group can be a good way of meeting people. You'll need a good working knowledge of Spanish for this, and you may be regarded as an eccentric at first, but you'll learn a lot as well as making friends. If you've got a skill you can contribute to the group, all the better.

## WHAT TO WEAR

A combination of warm climate and scarce resources means that dress in Cuba is usually very informal by European or North American standards. Men sometimes wear tropical-weight suits or jackets at business meetings or official events, but it is fine to wear a shirt and tie or a *guayabera*—a classic Cuban shirt. Said to have originated in central Cuba, where workers picking guavas (*guayabas*) needed pockets to hold the fruit, it has short or long sleeves, two or four patch pockets, decorative vertical bands on the front, and mother-of pearl buttons. It's designed to be worn loose, and is acceptable on even the most formal of occasions.

Cuban women are very careful about their appearance and tend to dress less informally than men both at the office and in the evening. Trousers are usually acceptable. For both men and women, shorts are worn only at the beach or around the house. On the whole, the watchword for the visitor is well-groomed informality. It is never tactful to dress with ostentatious expense.

## CONVERSATIONS
### Politics

You are almost certain to be asked, "Do you like Cuba?" and you should *not* treat this as an invitation to launch into a detailed critique of the government or its leaders. People's responses to recent history are both passionate and ambiguous, and you will hear polarized and often contradictory views. Don't press anyone to talk about the political situation, and, particularly, don't solicit their views on Fidel. When in doubt, listen rather than speak. If you initiate a conversation, it should deal with neutral topics or the kind of things Cubans can feel unequivocally proud of, such as the music, film, sports, or natural beauty of the country.

That said, some of those who want to talk to you will be people critical of the government or marginalized in some way, who feel it is easier to express their opinions to foreigners than to other Cubans. They may seem paranoid: someone who is pouring out their soul to you may clam up if another Cuban appears, particularly someone they don't know.

This raises the vexed question of spying. Ironically for such a talkative nation, secrecy is endemic to Cuban society, for good reason. It cannot be denied that state security watches the population and especially suspected dissidents, and by expressing or inviting strong critical opinions in conversation with Cubans you could make them suspect. Ordinary tourists are unlikely to have a spy or "minder" keeping an eye on them, but people visiting Cuba for professional or business purposes—and particularly journalists— might well be under quiet surveillance. The wisest approach in conversation is to be politically discreet and noncommittal.

## Liaisons Dangereuses?

Sex and love are often the subject of conversations and gossip, and getting to know people of the opposite sex can be a flirtatious process, but it's all generally treated with a light touch. Remember, however, that Cubans tend to apply different rules to themselves and to tourists. Sex tourism, unfortunately, has rubbed off on to all tourism, and Cubans may think you are expecting sex. So, whether you're a man or a woman, it probably won't be long before you are propositioned—but beware, your new squeeze will probably want a tradeoff in terms of money, possessions ("You will leave me that watch when you go, won't you?"), or even the chance to leave the country. It is not unknown for a Cuban to seek to marry a foreign visitor in order to leave Cuba legally.

As everywhere in Latin America, women (both Cuban and foreign) get ceaseless attention from men. This rarely amounts to sexual harassment, however, and flirtatious approaches are usually easy to sidestep or ignore. One such is the *piropo*, the equivalent of the construction-site whistle. In the past it is said to have been rather more gallant than the crude whispers you may hear—if you have the Spanish to understand them—though occasionally an elderly gent may make an elegant compliment or witty remark. Unless you want to plunge into Cuban gender relations at the deep end, the best response to the *piropo* is to do and say nothing. You simply didn't hear it.

## ESCAPING THE TOURIST ENCLAVES

Most people will pay their first and possibly their only visit to Cuba as a tourist. But there are many ways you can experience the country apart from the standard sunshine and seaside vacation package, which offers you little escape from tourist enclaves. Here are a few of them.

### Roads Less Traveled

Specialist educational and solidarity-based tours are a good way of visiting Cuba. Over forty companies in the U.K. and Ireland, and many others in continental Europe and the Antipodes, offer tours focusing on Afro-Cuba, outdoor or cultural activities, and the history and achievements of the Revolution.

U.S. citizens are still effectively prohibited by their government from visiting Cuba as tourists, but can obtain a license for specific purposes (government business, visits from international organizations, noncommercial research, or journalism). Increasingly U.S. citizens travel to Cuba via a third country; they risk a big fine if caught on return by U.S. immigration officials, and the Bush administration's attitude to Cuba holds out no promise of easing these restrictions. Anyone applying for a license or a visa must do so through the Cuban Interests Section in Washington, D.C.

It's more challenging—but by no means impossible, and potentially more rewarding—to go as an individual traveler, as long as you have fairly confident Spanish, and are willing to spend time on making the arrangements. Many Europeans are doing this, for instance adding Cuba to a self-organized journey around Latin America. To enter Cuba, citizens of most countries need only their passport, return tickets, and a thirty-day tourist card (not strictly speaking a visa, this is a separate paper that the Cuban immigration official stamps instead of your passport; you hand it in on departure). They should also have evidence that they are staying in hotels, but in practice people often make hotel bookings (which appear on their tourist card) but stay with friends or in private houses (*casas particulares*). A good approach could be to stay in a neighborhood and get to know it and the people who live there, traveling in local buses rather than taxis, instead of staying cocooned in a resort. Tourist traps can be just that. The government may want you to stay in a tourist resort and spend money there, but the inquiring mind will inevitably seek something more.

**Volunteering**

If you want to do something useful during your stay, you can join one of the innumerable brigades and work–study tours organized by Cuba solidarity campaigns and friendship associations. Such organizations exist in over a hundred countries, including the United States, so there will almost certainly be one near you. Brigades spend periods from a few weeks to a few months helping out in agriculture, building, or other activities, and the experience always includes educational visits and quite a lot of music and dancing in the evenings. The solidarity-brigade approach, however, is one of unconditional support, not critical analysis of the Revolution. Church groups also organize solidarity tours, usually from a humanitarian or charity angle rather than one of uncritical political solidarity, but in recognition of the advances toward social justice the Revolution has achieved.

**STAYING LONGER**

Of course, the best way to get to know a country and its people is to live there, and work or study. Doing this in Cuba is not necessarily easy, and a lot of bureaucracy is involved—for instance, you will need an invitation and a visa specific to your purpose—but it is possible.

Cuba offers a variety of study opportunities: specialist institutes offer film and television, music, dance, and other performing arts, Afro-Cuban studies, and even medicine. Courses in various subjects are also available at the University of Havana. If you need to learn Spanish first, you can do that too. Short courses are available at Havana and Santiago universities and there are some language schools. If you are undertaking relevant research you can also arrange to visit Cuba for that purpose.

If you want to work in Cuba, you cannot just arrive and scout around. The government contracts workers from abroad for certain skills in short supply on the island, but getting such work is a long bureaucratic process and you need an existing contact in Cuba who knows what jobs are available for foreigners and can steer you in the right direction. It is worth pointing out, too, that even two or three months as a member of a volunteer brigade cannot prepare a person from a wealthy industrialized country for the challenges and hardships of living in resource-poor Cuba for a long time.

# chapter six

# TIME OUT

Cubans enjoy their leisure time with just as much energy as they put into work. Cinema and the performing arts are cheap and well-attended; making music and listening and dancing to it are national obsessions; but, since the climate is near perfect and money often short, Cubans also spend much of their free time in parks, on beaches, in open-air ice-cream parlors, or at home, playing chess or dominoes, or indulging in their favorite pastime—conversation.

**MONEY MATTERS**

Currency is highly confusing for the visitor, not least because the rules keep changing (see Chapter 1, Economy). The national currency (*moneda nacional*) is the peso. Since October 25, 2004, Cuba has replaced the U.S. dollar with the Cuban convertible peso (CUC) as the official currency for tourists (although Cubans can use CUC too, if they can get hold of them). Tourists can no longer use dollars, but they can use the ordinary Cuban peso. The CUC is not an international currency, and has value only within Cuba (remember to change back your remaining CUC before leaving the country). In 2005 its value was set at U.S. $1.08. Everyone entering with U.S. dollars must change them into Cuban convertible pesos on arrival; in fact it is better to change dollars into another currency beforehand, since an extra 10 percent fee is charged on exchanges of U.S. cash for CUC in the country. Most currencies can be exchanged for CUC or ordinary pesos.

Money is changed legally in banks and *casas de cambio* (CADECAs). It is unwise to change money on the street, however good the rate looks. The main Cuban banks have branches throughout the country, and many have outlets in hotels. Banks normally operate Monday to Friday, 8:00 a.m. to 3:00 p.m., although the hours are often extended in tourist areas and in Havana, and many CADECAs are open twenty-four hours a day.

Foreigners pay for almost everything in CUC, although an ever-increasing number of places accept either CUC or pesos, and euros are increasingly accepted in tourist-oriented outlets. It is not uncommon to pay in CUC and receive change in pesos. You will need pesos mainly for purchases at markets, street stalls or kiosks, local bus fares, books or newspapers, or cinema tickets.

The symbol for the ordinary Cuban peso is $, just as for the U.S. dollar—another source of confusion. Pesos and CUC come in similar denominations, but peso notes bear portraits of national heroes, whereas CUC notes are newer and have pictures of national monuments. CUC coins bear the inscription INTUR. Street scams often rely on visitors' ignorance of the differences between currencies. Always check your change.

Traveler's checks in Canadian dollars, sterling, or euros are valid unless they are issued by U.S. banks. Commissions range between 2 and 4 percent. You can withdraw money using a non-U.S. credit card, but debit cards such as Maestro are problematic. ATMs are increasing in number, but are still rare outside major cities and not very reliable. Non-U.S. credit cards are accepted in most places; but American Express and even Visa cards issued in the United States are nowhere acceptable. It is usually simpler just to have cash.

## SHOPPING

Cuba is not a consumer society. The range of goods in shops is severely restricted by state control of the economy, a scarcity of hard currency, and the U.S. embargo. When new goods arrive they are snapped up instantly. Cubans have ration cards for food and some other items, but they do not guarantee all the basic essentials.

There are no fixed opening times for shops; it's best to find out by asking someone. There are air-conditioned stores, often attached to hotels, that cater to visitors and accept CUC or credit cards. They sell travel items such as insect repellent, along with such recommended purchases as rum, coffee, cigars, and recorded music. Other CUC shops are aimed at local custom, for those with access to CUC or hard currency. However, free-market peso stores are improving their quality and range to compete with these outlets. The reintroduction of private enterprise has boosted food and handicraft markets, and stallholders now accept CUC as well as *moneda nacional*, though change will usually be in the latter.

The farmers markets, usually open on Sunday mornings as well as Tuesday through Friday, are lively and entertaining, the most famous being Havana's Mercado de Cuatro Caminos.

Some fine art is sold at galleries, but you need a special license and certificate of authenticity to take artworks out of the country. The secondhand book market in Havana's Plaza de Armas is an excellent place to pick up out-of-print Cuban classics. Handicraft markets sell tacky souvenirs.

## CUBAN CIGARS

Cuba produces the best cigars in the world, in a huge range of types and sizes. A highly labor-intensive crop, tobacco is grown mostly on small farms, principally in Vuelta Abajo and Semi-Vuelta in Pinar del Río province and in parts of central Cuba. Tobacco workers were traditionally in the vanguard of the Cuban labor movement.

Cigar sales suffered for many years from the U.S. embargo, and a large black market has evolved. It is best to buy at state-run Casas del Habano. Make sure the box bears the label *hecho in Cuba totalmente a mano* (totally handmade in Cuba), the official government seal, and the "Habanos" band. If not, the cigars are not genuine. Cigars labeled *Bauza* do not meet the required standards but are still of good quality. Avoid street hustlers selling inferior cigars.

## EATING OUT

Few people visit Cuba for the food. Cubans, on the other hand, take tours in their own country precisely for the food, where quantity, not quality, is the watchword, and where they will be able to eat large amounts of foods normally rationed. Prerevolutionary cuisine, for the rich at least, was sophisticated and varied; but the Revolution's struggle to provide enough food for everyone has cut the Cuban diet very much down to size. Eating out is therefore something of a challenge.

Vegetarians will have trouble outside hotel restaurants: it is puzzling that with such a good climate for horticulture Cubans have so little interest in vegetables. Meat is considered the *raison d'être* of a meal. A perennial favorite is *lechón con yuca*—roast suckling pig with yucca. Vegetable garnishes are usually fried plantain or a simple salad, dessert may be a tropical fruit salad or a combination of sweet guava paste (*dulce de guayaba*) with cheese. Alternatively, you can eat your dessert in an ice-cream parlor; the best and most famous is Coppelia in Havana, where the long, gossipy line is part of the experience.

International and fast-food restaurants are also springing up everywhere, but the food is bland and monotonous. Unfortunately, the service and ambience in many restaurants are unimpressive, though the state-run ones have improved with the onslaught of tourism and some are housed in beautifully restored colonial buildings. Some upscale restaurants require male guests to wear a jacket and tie. Be prepared for staff to be truculent and unhelpful, a legacy of the time when they received no tips and had no incentive to be polite.

Cheaper, and in many ways more interesting, are the informal-economy *paladares*, small family-run restaurants, often in private houses or apartments, which may serve up to twelve diners. They are quite highly regulated, though the rules are creatively interpreted. Check prices first, and if there is no written menu and price list, beware. There may be several menus listing similar dishes at different prices, the foreigner being presented with the most expensive version. If someone leads you to a *paladar*, be aware that their commission will be incorporated into your bill.

Except in Havana, few restaurants serve dinner after 10:00 p.m. Restaurants and *paladares* expect to be paid in CUC; only the better restaurants and hotels accept credit cards. Air-conditioning can be very chilly, so take a light sweater.

---

### TIPPING

Perhaps surprisingly, everyone, from the doorman at the hotel through washroom and car park attendants to wandering musicians, will expect a tip. A tour guide will expect around 2 CUC per person and taxi drivers 10 percent of the meter fare—but do not tip if you have negotiated a fare without a meter. The usual restaurant tip is 10 percent in the same currency in which you have paid the bill, though in *paladares* (see above) the tip is usually incorporated into the bill.

## DRINKS

It's the drinks, and particularly its rum-based cocktails, for which Cuba is famous. Beer (*cerveza*) is drunk very cold and at any time of the day. Cristal (light) and Bucanero (strong) are popular varieties. There are various soft drinks (*refrescos*). Coffee is always strong and usually has sugar already added—ask for *sin azúcar* if you don't take sugar, *cortado* for a dash of milk, and *café con leche* for a latte.

Forget tea, although chamomile (*manzanilla*) tea is fairly common. Cuba produces wine under the Soroa label, but imported wine is better.

### Cocktails with History

Rum is the basis for all Cuba's well-known cocktails: the *mojito* (white rum, lime juice, and a sprig of mint), the *daiquiri* (named after Daiquirí near Santiago, where it was invented in the early 1900s), and the *Cuba libre*, combining rum with that byword for U.S. domination, Coca-Cola. The Cuba Libre was reputedly invented by U.S. soldiers during the 1898 independence war, the name deriving from the nationalists' motto, "Free Cuba." You can sample these drinks pretty much anywhere. Two famous places in Havana to do so are the Bodeguita

del Medio, its walls covered in
signatures and autographed pictures
of its famous patrons, and the Floridita,
Ernest Hemingway's favorite haunt—but
they are more frequented by tourists than
locals nowadays.

## THE ARTS
### Culture and Censorship

By providing universal education, the revolution
made many forms of culture accessible to all
Cubans for the first time. Popular culture, and in
particular the music and dance that have become
world-famous, had of course existed for centuries,
but the revolution saw a great flowering of culture
in which museums and art galleries were opened,
orchestras, dance and theater groups, and art
schools sprang into existence, and a vibrant
national film industry was born. Local cultural
centers, or *Casas de la Cultura*, where people can
take evening classes, join a choir or a municipal
band, hear concerts, and watch movies, were
created nationwide. The *Casa de las Américas*,
founded in 1960, has grown into one of Latin
America's most prestigious cultural institutions,
awarding annual literary, musical, and artistic
prizes and holding conferences, exhibitions, and
concerts. There are national institutes for writers,

artists, and the cinema. Creative artists in Cuba are employed by the state; they don't have to wait tables or work in shops to fund their art, waiting for the "big break," though teaching may be an integral part of their jobs.

Yet censorship and discrimination remain. Political censorship has attracted the strongest international disapproval, partly through the publicity given to high-profile exiles. However, it could be argued that while the Revolution penalizes the writing of certain opinions, without it most Cubans would not be able to write even their own names.

As in many areas of Cuban life, contradictions abound. The Revolution at first promoted intellectual freedom and artistic creativity, but the siege mentality generated by the Bay of Pigs set strict boundaries on freedom of expression. In his 1961 "Speech to the Intellectuals," Castro made one of his most-quoted pronouncements: "Within the Revolution, everything, against the Revolution nothing . . . We don't tell anyone what to write about . . . but we will always judge their literary work through the prism of the Revolution." The Soviet-influenced 1970s was the toughest decade for intellectual freedom, but also produced impressive works in all the arts. There has been a marked relaxation in prejudice and censorship since the 1990s and, overall, Cuban intellectual life is one of Latin America's richest.

## Attending Events

Hotels, travel agents, and airports distribute information about forthcoming cultural events. Foreigners are not expected to stand in line, and can buy tickets at tourist agencies and hotels, or from Agencia Paradiso, the agency specializing in cultural tourism.

## Music and Dance

Music and dance are Cuba's lifeblood. Especially since 1996, when U.S. singer-guitarist Ry Cooder assembled an ad hoc group of veteran Cuban musicians as the Buena Vista Social Club, Cuban popular music and jazz have become the island's most visible and successful export and the focus of several international festivals held in Cuba.

Scarcely influenced by commercialism, Cuban popular music is the fruit of an unbroken tradition. The style now familiar worldwide is a fusion of several traditional genres: the *décima*, in which couplets or short stanzas alternate competitively; the country music *punto guajiro*, whose most famous example is Joseíto Fernandez's *Guantanamera*, written in 1929; and the French- and Spanish-influenced *danzón*, which evolved during the 1920s into the linchpin of Cuban music, the *son*. The famous offshoot of the *son* is the *rumba*, which merges the *décima* with African rhythms. These traditional forms are the basis and forerunners of modern salsa and Cuban jazz, and new generations of *soneros* both in and outside Cuba continue to develop them.

While these musical forms predate the Revolution, the late 1960s produced the *nueva trova*, a popular school of singer-songwriters who explicitly supported the Revolution. Its leading figures are Silvio Rodríguez and Pablo Milanés and its lyrics both praise and criticize Cuban society while celebrating the ideals of the Revolution.

Cuba also has a body of classical music going back to the eighteenth-century Church music composer Esteban Salas, and has several contemporary exponents, such as the composer–guitarist Leo Brouwer. There is a national symphony orchestra and a national choir, and several chamber ensembles and choirs.

Many Havana hotels stage concerts featuring top bands. Not all performances are advertised, so ask around. The most enjoyable performances are ad hoc, when amateur musicians gather at a local *casa de la trova*—every town has one, and Santiago has a whole street, the Calle Heredia. There are *cumbanchas* (street parties), and live music in cafés, bars, and hotels. Classical venues in Havana include the Teatro Amadeo Roldán and the Basilica de San Francisco de Asís.

Dance seems the natural body language of all Cubans! There are two principal national dance companies—the Ballet Nacional de Cuba, founded in 1948 by the prima ballerina Alicia Alonso, and the Conjunto Folklórico Nacional de Cuba, founded in 1962 to celebrate traditional and Afro-Cuban dance. There is also the Ballet de Camagüey, and there are several modern dance companies.

Among many opportunities to see dance performances, the Conjunto Folklórico Nacional gives a *rumba* performance every Saturday in Havana, while the Ballet Nacional de Cuba performs year-round at the Gran Teatro de La Habana and organizes an annual ballet festival.

**Cinema and Theater**
Cuban cinema is another of the glories of the Revolution, made possible by the founding in 1959 of the Cuban film institute ICAIC. The

1960s was a golden age in Cuban cinema, culminating in 1968, the year of Tomás Gutiérrez Alea's *Memorias del Subdesarrollo* (*Memories of Underdevelopment*) and Humberto Solás's *Lucia*; but world-class films continue to appear despite economic constraints. Since the Special Period Cuba's cinema industry has increasingly relied on foreign investment, and this may influence the shift away from didactic or message-based films. Each December Havana hosts the major Festival Internacional del Cine Latinoamericano.

The scope for criticizing aspects of the Revolution has fluctuated. Gutiérrez Alea satirized government bureaucracy from "inside" the Revolution in his films from 1966 to 1995; unswerving in his commitment to the Revolution, he was inspired by the contradictions within it.

Cubans love the cinema, and virtually everybody can afford it, so lines are long. Listings are published in local newspapers and on posters. Remember that films are not subtitled in English.

Before the Revolution Cuba had fewer than fifteen theaters, but now there are over sixty, and Havana hosts a biennial international theater festival. All the main cities offer mainstream and experimental productions. Teatro Cabildo in Santiago and El Público in Havana have their own permanent theaters. Teatro Escambray, founded in 1968 as a community-based theater in the rural zones of the Escambray Mountains, is still active in both performance and teaching.

## Visual Arts

Many of the painters who define the national artistic idiom, such as Wifredo Lam (1902–82) and René Portocarrero (1912–85), predate the Revolution but embraced it. After 1959 a program of art education was developed and the National School of Art and the Institute for Advanced Art Studies were founded. Castro ignored fine art, but never actually restricted it, which meant that it was not reduced to political propaganda. Graphic arts, however, became an essential channel for revolutionary messages, and tremendous creativity went into posters and murals.

Now the government enthusiastically promotes Cuban art. Galleries are state-run, and works may be bought through them. Recent generations of Cuban artists, including Manuel Mendive, whose work is based on Yoruba myths and traditions, and Flora Fong, have achieved international recognition. Exhibitions such as the Havana Biennial, held in November in odd-numbered years, help to promote the work of young artists.

For gallery events, consult the free publication *Arte en La Habana*. Some of Cuba's best works from the contemporary and earlier periods can be viewed in Havana's Museo Nacional de Bellas Artes.

## Literature and Books

Books in Cuba are abundant and cheap. The state publishing industry is at the service of education, and reading is vigorously promoted. Fidel is a famously avid reader. Glossy production values are almost absent, but the range of Cuban and Latin American works and translations of classics from other languages is astonishing. Even during the worst of the Special Period, books were printed, on newsprint, using presses imported when the Soviet economy was collapsing. Each January or February there is an International Book Fair in Havana, which then tours the island.

Questions of national identity and social problems have always featured in Cuban literature: the works of José Martí arc a classic example and slavery was a favorite subject of nineteenth-century novels. The postrevolutionary period tapped into this and genres such as crime fiction are a relatively recent development. Cubans are fond of poetry, so don't be surprised if someone quotes verses at you.

The best-known Cuban books in the West tend to be by exiled authors criticizing the regime or dealing with formerly taboo subjects. But there are many more writers who celebrate the Revolution and its values, such as the poet Nicolás Guillén, who became a laureate in the early revolutionary period, and the author Alejo Carpentier, a key exponent of "magical realism."

## MUSEUMS

Cuba is a country of museums. There are museums devoted to everything from music to tobacco, cars to colonial and local history. Many are set in colonial buildings that are treasures in themselves. The oldest museum was founded in 1899 in Santiago by the son of the founder of the Bacardí rum distillery.

Museum opening times are a law unto themselves, and unreliable even if advertised. Mondays or Tuesdays are official closing days. Many larger museums charge entrance fees and an extra fee for photography. Some museums have guided tours as part of the package. Signs and labels are usually written only in Spanish.

## SPORTS AND OUTDOOR ACTIVITIES

Although professional sporting activity was abolished after the Revolution, large resources have been invested in amateur sports. Castro views sports as an integral part of education, and they are seen as a source of national pride and an advertisement for the Revolution.

Baseball (*beisbol*) and boxing are the most popular sports. Baseball arrived from the U.S.A. in the 1860s and is now, ironically, the national game. Cuba won the first-ever Olympic gold in baseball at the 1992 Barcelona games. Matches are well worth attending, even if just for the atmosphere. The larger stadiums have reserved seating areas for foreigners, but it's more fun to mingle with the Cuban spectators.

Cuba has won several Olympic boxing titles, Teófilo Stevenson being especially revered. Two athletic Olympians are Alberto Juantorena and María Colón. All were at their peak in the 1970s.

Other major sports played in Cuba include volleyball, basketball, and, increasingly, football. In rural areas cockfighting is common but illegal. Chess games are a common sight on front stoops and in parks, and sultry evenings often resound to the clack of dominoes and the clink of rum-filled glasses.

Mass tourism has opened the floodgates for outdoor pursuits. Diving, surfing, and game fishing are favorites. The waters off the Isla de la Juventud provide one of the world's great diving sites. Most holiday villages have tennis courts, and some their own golf courses. Cycling, walking, and trekking on horseback are growing activities. The Sierra Maestra and the Topes de Collantes, near Trinidad, are beautiful hiking areas. Hikes to the mountaintops require a guide, but unguided low-level trails are being developed, as are specialist ecotourism programs for bird-watchers, botanists, and cavers.

## SEX
### Prostitution

Brothels and prostitution were outlawed by the Revolution, but they continued to exist secretly. Now prostitution has resurfaced; it is illegal, but the government often turns a blind eye for economic reasons. The sex trade flourishes in streets, hotel lobbies, and tourist bars. The struggle to make ends meet has forced many women into occasional prostitution. An unfortunate side effect is the growth of sex tourism involving minors and catering to a market of middle-aged white Western men; it is both illegal and dangerous.

Prostitutes have been claimed to be employed as spies for the government.

## The Gay Scene

Life for homosexuals in Cuba is uneasy, but a big improvement on the 1960s, when homosexuality was a prison offence, and even the 1980s, when homosexuals could not be teachers. Official intolerance gradually faded during the 1990s, especially following the release of Gutiérrez Alea's 1993 film *Fresa y Chocolate* ("Strawberry and Chocolate"), the story of a gay man and a young communist. In 2001 the first (nonlegal) gay marriages took place.

Gay Cubans still may not join the Communist Party, and public display of homosexual behavior is illegal. There are no public venues where gay people can socialize, so much of the gay scene takes place in private homes. Unofficial prejudice against homosexuals persists.

## DRUGS

Illegal drug use among Cubans is lower than in the developed countries. Many young Cubans smoke marijuana, much of it originating in Jamaica, but it's also homegrown, especially around Guantánamo. Hustlers try to sell marijuana to tourists, but beware: foreigners found in possession of illegal drugs will be deported and there are long prison sentences for dealing.

# GETTING AROUND

The "three Rs" to remember when traveling in Cuba are rules, regulations, and requirements. These are unlikely to make travel fast or easy. Fuel shortages and lack of spare parts crippled public transportation in the mid 1990s, but the system has improved and become more reliable in recent years, not least because of the tourist industry.

As with many other aspects of Cuba, there is one set of Rs for foreigners and another for Cubans, applying to currency, ticketing, and sometimes the actual vehicles available.

## LINE MANAGEMENT

In Cuba, *cola* is usually not a brown fizzy drink but the ubiquitous line, or queue. Unless you always travel by tourist-only transportation or in a car, it won't be long before you find yourself standing in a *cola* waiting for a bus or buying a ticket. It usually looks more like a loose crowd of people than a line, but when you arrive at the stop, or in the waiting room, you call out "*¿El último?*" ("Who's the last in line?"), whereupon the last arrival in the *cola* before you identifies him or herself and you become *el último*, and must identify yourself to the next person. Although the *cola* usually forms itself into a line when the bus arrives, sometimes (if it's hot, or wet, or the bus is very late) it degenerates into a scramble. On the plus side, kindly Cubans may push you to the head of the *cola*, which you should accept graciously, however you may feel.

## LONG-DISTANCE TRAVEL
### Trains

The state railway company, Ferrocarriles de Cuba, serves Havana and the provincial capitals. If you are not in a hurry and don't fancy *colas*, the train is a good option. It is safe and comfortable, and getting a ticket is normally easy. Foreigners can book in advance at the larger hotels or through Ferrotur offices or the LADIS agency, and must pay in CUC. In smaller towns and for local trains you will have to join the *cola* at the station ticket office at least two hours before the train is due. Boarding without a ticket attracts a 100 percent surcharge. Expect delays and cancellations— timetables at stations are optimistic.

There are three classes of train. *Especiales,* fast trains joining Havana and Santiago (also known as the *tren francés*—the French train —because this service now uses old Trans-Europe Express coaches bought from France in 2001), have reclining seats, nonsmoking cars, a buffet service, and vicious air-conditioning. Bring your own toilet paper, however.

Most trains are classed as r*egular* (don't be misled; this means "ordinary," not "regular"). They are slower and have neither nonsmoking cars nor air-conditioning, but the windows can be opened. Not all have a buffet service. Trains classed as *lecheros* (literally "milk trains") are really basic, stopping at every hamlet. All interprovincial trains depart from Havana's Estación de Ferrocarril.

Taking the astonishingly slow "Hershey train" (so named because the tracks were laid by the American chocolate firm) between Havana and Matanzas is a charming day out. Cuba's only electric train, it ambles through lush greenery past sugar mills. Take the bus back!

**Buses**

Most tourists travel around on tour buses: not a cheap option but a comfortable one, which can be arranged at short notice. Information and timetables are usually available in hotel lobbies.

The state company Astro provides a service both for locals (who pay in pesos) and foreigners (who pay in CUC), though only a few tickets are available for CUC on most departures. Standbys (*fallos*) can be bought at the last minute. Astro serves virtually every town in the country, but many services run only on alternate days and some leave in the middle of the night. Scheduled departures are liable to change at the last minute. For a higher fare, Viazul offers a more reliable, punctual, and comfortable service (foreigners only), with toilets and glacial air-conditioning but serving only major towns and tourist spots. Havana's Viazul terminal is a taxi journey from the city center. Although refreshment stops are frequent, it's advisable to take your own food. Reboard promptly, or you may lose your seat.

Travel on local buses is very cheap (payable in pesos), but you can't make reservations. Local services are often run by provincial enterprises and you may have to change services at provincial boundaries and buy a fresh ticket. Expect to spend a lot of time in the *cola*. You'll be put on a list or given a number. Wait to be called, but don't wander off, or you may find yourself at the end of the *cola*. Be alert for scams, such as being told the wrong departure time  for your bus, so that you miss it and the ticket seller then tries to sell you a seat in a private taxi.

### Trucks

Open trucks (*camiones*), minimally converted for passengers, are an uncomfortable, but cheap and relatively fast way to travel between provinces. There are departure points in every city, and the trucks run to a (fairly loose) schedule. Payment, made as you board, is a fraction of the bus fare. An excellent way of meeting local people!

### Taxis

Long-distance taxis can be found at train stations and interprovincial bus stations. They have fixed routes (often painted on the hoods) and leave only when they are full, which can mean a wait. However, they do offer an alternative to the bus ticket *cola*. State-owned CUC taxis (*colectivos*) are faster and sometimes cheaper than buses. State-owned peso taxis (*máquinas*) are not allowed to take foreigners, but often do. Private taxis (*particulares*) are cheaper than most other taxis. Some are metered but you will need to negotiate a price before departure. At police checkpoints drivers will be fined if they carry foreigners illicitly or have not paid their license to operate, but fines are often built into the fare anyway.

### Air

Cuba is an unlikely pioneer in air travel. The International Air Transport Association (IATA) was founded in Havana in 1945, and Cubana is one of the oldest airlines in the world. Nowadays it uses Airbus planes on most of its international routes. However, much of the domestic fleet now consists of old Russian Antonovs, some converted from freight to passenger use.

Alternatives are Aerocaribbean (smaller, older aircraft with strict weight limits) and Aerotaxi, which flies charters (usually four seaters; you have to rent the entire plane) to smaller airports around Cuba. Buy tickets at hotel tour desks and travel agencies rather than at airline offices, which are invariably chaotic. It is also very difficult to book flights from one city to another when not at the point of departure, except from Havana.

Since 1998 there has been increased competition from a new airline, Inter, an offshoot of the Central American TACA.

**Car Rental**

To rent a car you will need to show a valid driver's license or an international license, be over the age of twenty-one with a valid passport, and leave a deposit in cash or an imprint of a non-U.S. credit card. No international car companies operate in Cuba but the usual car rental procedures apply with the national ones. Check the car for any damage predeparture, and beware of additional charges that suddenly appear on your bill when you return it. It's advisable to take out optional insurance for rental cars to cover accidents and theft. There is a penalty charge if you lose your car rental contract, and if you are involved in an accident you must get a copy of the police report (*denuncia*) and hand it to the car rental company to be eligible for the insurance coverage.

Gasoline is available at Cupet stations (*servicentros*, commonly known as *servis*). There

are two grades, *especial* and *regular*, but foreigners will only be served *especial*. *Servis* often form the central hub of small towns and are open twenty-four hours a day. Outside the towns there are very few gas stations. A good road map is essential. The *Mapa Turístico de Cuba*, although not the best, indicates the locations of Cupet stations.

In response to the transportation crisis, Cubans have taken to organized hitchhiking. At major junctions away from city centers, traffic lights, and rail crossings, people known as *amarillos* organize *colas* and stop vehicles to find out their destinations. This is legal, and can be useful to foreign drivers unfamiliar with an area. It is best for foreign hitchhikers to travel in pairs.

Road conditions are bad in general, and night driving is particularly hazardous.

## Rules of the Road

Cubans officially drive on the right, but don't always adhere to this on country roads; in any case potholes can make it impossible. Speed limits are 31 mph (50 kmph) in urban areas, 56 mph (90 kmph) on open roads, with some areas restricted to 37 mph (60 kmph), and 62–75 mph (100–120 kmph) on highways (*autopistas*). However, Cubans often drive as fast as their vehicle will allow, which is, fortunately, usually not very fast. There are on-the-spot fines for speeding, and speed traps are common on the *autopista*. There is no law on seat belts, which are generally fitted only in officially rented cars. The official blood/alcohol limit is 80mg/100ml, and there is a hefty on-the-spot fine for foreigners caught drunk driving.

If you encounter a *punta de control* (police checkpoint), you must stop. Sentry boxes are installed at most major intersections. A sign saying "*pare*," a red upside-down triangle inside a red circle, means "Stop," not "Give way," which is "*ceda el paso*" in a red upside-down triangle on a yellow background. Standard international road signs are in use, but sporadically, and directional signs are often obscure or missing.

If you are involved in an accident, do not move your vehicle, or allow any other vehicle involved to be moved. Take all relevant details and call the transit police. If someone is seriously injured or killed you must contact your embassy. If you are held responsible for the accident, the police can confiscate your passport so that you cannot leave the country.

### Bicycles and Motorcycles

Until the 1990s bicycles were not seen as a serious form of urban transportation, and anyone riding one to work was regarded as a complete eccentric. The Special Period changed all that, and bicycles now outnumber cars 20:1, and there are bike lanes and bike workshops everywhere.

Bicycle rental is rare, and mainly in the Havana area, so foreigners often bring their own. Bring a helmet, too, and a chain and padlock, and always use dedicated bicycle parks. Ambushing cyclists, especially in quiet streets at night, is common.

There are few motorcycle facilities, but scooters and mopeds can be rented in many resorts.

### Ferries

Ferries and hydrofoils serve the Isla de la Juventud from Suridero de Batabano on the southern coast. Cubanacán also runs brand-new catamarans that can convey up to 400 passengers between Varadero and Havana. Small ferries connect the coast north of Pinar del Río with Cayo Levisa.

## IN THE CITY

Cuban cities are mostly laid out on a grid pattern. Parallel streets (*calles*) are crossed by avenues (*avenidas*). In some cities streets and avenues are named and in others numbered or lettered, usually in a regular pattern that makes it easy to navigate. Every city has a central *plaza* or *parque*. Some streets retain their prerevolutionary names alongside the new ones introduced in 1959, which can be confusing. When asked, locals usually overestimate the time you need to walk anywhere.

The most comfortable—but most insulated—way of getting around cities is by taxi  Unsurprisingly, there are taxis for foreigners (charging in CUC) and taxis for Cubans. Tourist taxi stands are in front of all major hotels, at airports, and at strategic points around cities, but taxis can also be ordered by telephone or hailed in the street. Most taxis are metered, the money going to the state, but many drivers will offer the foreigner a flat, off-meter rate that the driver then pockets. Other unconventional forms of city transport are egg-shaped three-seater motor scooters, *cocotaxis*, rickshaws, *bicitaxis*, and horse-drawn cabs, *coches*—picturesque but pricey.

City buses, known as *guaguas*, are invariably overcrowded and hot and may be targeted by pickpockets. They ply fixed routes but you will need to know your way around to use them confidently. Inventive responses to the fuel crisis are the *ciclobus*, which carries passengers together with their bicycles, and, in Havana, a large, unwieldy semitrailer bus nicknamed with dry Cuban wit the *camello* (camel). The urban bus fare throughout Cuba is a flat rate of less than a peso. *Lanchas* are waterbuses that serve the communities around the bay areas of Havana, Santiago, and Cienfuegos.

Driving is as "interesting" in the city as on the open road, mostly because of obsolete or faulty lights and signage. It is often not clear who has priority at intersections. An important rule to remember is that you can turn right against a red light (being aware of cyclists and pedestrians as you do so) where you see the sign *Derecha Con Luz Roja*. Some streets have been converted into bus and bicycle routes only. Parking is generally a free-for-all, but you must park on the left in one-way streets, and your car will be removed if you park in zones marked *Zona Oficial*. Most tourist hotels provide parking; if you do park on the street overnight, it's best to pay the hotel doorman to keep an eye on the car. Rental cars are particularly liable to theft, and are identifiable by the license plates, which are prefixed TUR.

## WHERE TO STAY

Before the Revolution, Cuba had some of the finest hotels in the world. It has now come full circle and, thanks to foreign investment, luxury hotels are reappearing in the beach resorts, and many of the old hotels and beautiful colonial buildings are being refurbished to international standards. The high priority put on international tourism as an income generator makes water and electricity outages (power cuts) less frequent in tourist establishments than elsewhere.

Hotels are classified by the international star system, though standards can vary widely within a star rating. Peak seasons are December to March and July to August. Finding a hotel room is rarely a problem, even late at night. Breakfast is not usually included in the price, unless you have prebooked. If you want to meet locals, stay in a less expensive hotel—the more stars a hotel has, the more likely it is to exclude Cubans. *Peso* hotels are for Cubans, and rooms are rarely available to foreigners, but many are now being converted for that purpose.

A good alternative to a hotel is to stay in a private house (*casa particular*). Those licensed for this display a sticker with two blue triangles and the inscription

*Arrendador Inscripto.* It is legal to stay with a Cuban family as long as they are registered taxpayers. If you stay at an illegal residence, the family will be fined if discovered.

Official campsites are springing up all over Cuba, consisting of basic cabin accommodation rather than tents and normally with a restaurant and a swimming pool. Casual pitching of tents or sleeping out on the beach or in a field is illegal.

## HEALTH

Generally, vaccinations are not required by Cuban immigration, but protection against hepatitis A, typhoid, polio, and tetanus is recommended. If you have come from or been through areas infected by yellow fever and cholera you will require a certificate of vaccination against these.

Cuba has an excellent health service, but health insurance is recommended. Health care is not free for visitors treated in international clinics or public hospitals. In Havana, the Ciro García Central Clinic caters to foreigners only and the Hermanos Ameijeiras hospital has special floors for foreigners. Servimed, a state-run but for-profit health system for foreigners, has many centers around Cuba. Foreigners are often allowed to go ahead of others in regular health facilities but will be expected to pay in cash. International hotels have a doctor on call and many have a pharmacy.

Pharmacies are generally poorly stocked and you should bring your own medicine, sunscreen, and cosmetics. International pharmacies are better stocked but are not in every town. Opening times are: *turno regular* 8:00 a.m. to 5:00 p.m. daily, *turno especial* 8:00 a.m. to 10:30 p.m., and *turno permanente*, open twenty-four hours.

The most common ailment to strike visitors is diarrhea, and the standard measures for avoiding this in a poor country are advisable. During outages (cuts) in water supply, water is delivered to hotels and the local population. Public toilets are not easy to find, but you can use those in restaurants or bars without having to buy anything. It is courteous to ask first, however, and you may have to pay an attendant.

You'll need protection against sunburn and heatstroke, particularly between May and October—the breeze on the beach is deceptive. Despite the heat, summer colds are common, almost certainly because of the contrast between the heat outdoors and the chilly, stale air-conditioning indoors.

Insects are more of a nuisance than a hazard. You will need to come to terms with sharing your room with various creepy-crawlies, especially in cheap hotels. Mosquitoes are the main menace, and although they do not carry malaria, they can make your evenings and nights a misery. Bring your o insect repellent and, if you plan to camp, a mosquito net.

Passive smoking in restaurants, hotels, and public transportation is hard to avoid. Cuba is beginning to take measures against smoking, but very few restaurants have nonsmoking areas and any "no smoking" signs are blithely ignored.

## CRIME AND SAFETY

Cuba has little violent crime and is safer than many of its Caribbean and Latin American neighbors. In 1999 the government made it a serious crime to do anything to harm tourism. However, the economic crisis, together with tourism itself, has spawned begging and petty theft, especially in urban tourist areas. If you are a victim of crime, you are unlikely to be harmed. Take all the usual precautions, including leaving valuables in a hotel safety deposit box (*caja de seguridad*), not in your room. Despite the people on duty in CDRs on every other corner, take care while walking at night and avoid dark backstreets.

Hustlers (*jineteros/as*) trying to sell you something (sex, marijuana) or obtain something from you on the cheap (chiefly hard currency) have also, unfortunately, become a symbol of Cuba. Single women are favorite targets.

Most Cubans are kind and hospitable and many incidents of theft or hassle by *jineteros* are solved or averted by the intervention of passersby. Crimes should be reported to the Policía Nacional Revolucionaria (PNR), recognizable in the street by their blue trousers and light blue shirts. There is a special corps to protect tourists from pickpockets in tourist spots. They wear a dark blue uniform. Not all police speak English. If you are robbed, you should ask for a stamped statement (*denuncia*) for insurance purposes; in Havana, where thefts are commonest, the police will routinely issue one, but be prepared for a long wait at the police station.

It is illegal to take photographs of anything with a military connection, at airports, and even from an aircraft in Cuban airspace. It is also considered insensitive to take photographs of *colas*, although many Cubans love having their photograph taken. If in doubt, ask, but don't be surprised to be asked for money in exchange.

# BUSINESS BRIEFING

## THE ECONOMIC CLIMATE

Now that the Cuban government is actively seeking foreign investment, opportunities for doing business in Cuba abound. However, this is a country in gradual and careful economic transition, and two key points to remember from the outset are, first, that the legislation and regulations governing business relationships with foreign partners change fast and not necessarily predictably, and, second, that there is no point looking to Cuba for a quick buck—you will need a great deal of patience and willingness to build long-term business relationships.

Cuba now trades with many countries, even, to a limited extent, with the United States. The gradual growth in trade between the adversaries owes much to the work of the U.S.–Cuba Trade and Economic Council, a private nonprofit organization that asserts political neutrality in its promotion of trade between the two countries.

Spain, Canada, Italy, France, the United Kingdom, Mexico, Venezuela, and China are the main current investors in Cuba, in sectors including energy, financial services, mining, manufacturing, and IT as well as tourism. The government is inviting further investment in these and other sectors, including the modernization of various industries, transportation, construction materials, and biotechnology (in which Cuba is world-class). For a very specific range of products there are restrictions on exports to Cuba.

Cuba's first free-trade zone opened in 1997, and by 2005 four were in operation, in Havana Cienfuegos, the port of Mariel, and Wajay near the José Martí international airport.

Cuba organizes many international trade fairs. The Cuban Bureau of Conventions publishes a directory of the most important ones.

## CUBA AS A BUSINESS PARTNER

As a business partner, Cuba has advantages over most developing countries: a well-educated and qualified labor force able to assimilate new technologies rapidly, an adequate or updatable infrastructure, social stability, a generally crime-free environment safe for foreign personnel, and—as throughout its history—an economically strategic geographical location.

Corruption is reassuringly low. Offering sweeteners to officials will not benefit potential investors and could in fact harm their case. Transparency International, which monitors corruption worldwide, placed Cuba tenth in Latin America and the Caribbean in its 2004 Corruption Perceptions Index, below Chile and Brazil but above Mexico and Argentina.

Last but not least, as Cuba is not a member of any of the U.S.-dominated free-trade agreements in the Americas, non-U.S. investors have a competitive advantage in Cuba that they might not have in other Latin American countries.

However, recent economic recentralization measures have reduced the incentives for foreign investment since 2003. Cuba's current preference seems to be for a smaller number of larger projects in strategic sectors.

## GOVERNMENT AND BUSINESS

If you do business in Cuba, you will mostly be doing it with the government. The economy is still massively in state hands, the tiny private sector consisting almost entirely of small family businesses. Foreign companies can set up joint ventures or "mixed enterprises" (*empresas mixtas*) with Cuban government entities (see page 43); there are also "autonomous enterprises," which have boards and issue company reports. One hundred percent foreign ownership has been allowed since 1995, with some limitations. These companies differ from state enterprises in that they can make their own buying or investment decisions relatively independently of the state, but within government-set guidelines. They can also be registered outside Cuba. However, all these forms of association are ultimately connected to a Cuban government entity. You will need to get to know the precise relationship between the mixed or autonomous enterprise you are dealing with and the government entities involved.

Profits accruing to the government from any of these enterprises are plowed into social benefits such as subsidized food, transportation, education, and health care. It is important for a business proposal from a foreign entrepreneur to demonstrate tangible benefits to the Cuban people—by creating jobs, paying taxes, and expanding the economy. Entrepreneurs committed to environmental conservation and sustainable development are welcomed.

The Investment Promotion Center of the Ministry for Foreign Investment and Economic Cooperation (MINVEC) keeps a directory of business opportunities. Cuba's monthly magazine

*Business Tips on Cuba* also contains useful information on investment opportunities.

## THE LEGAL FRAMEWORK

The law in Cuba declares all economic sectors open to foreign investment apart from health care, education, and the armed forces (except their entrepreneurial arm, which counts as a national investor). The legislation emphasizes, however, that any mixed enterprises must contribute to the sustainable social and economic development of the country "on the basis of respect for the country's sovereignty and independence and the protection and rational use of natural resources."

Except for some technical and managerial posts, Cuban staff must be hired through the Cuban government employment agency, not directly by the mixed enterprise. There is specific legislation regulating investment in Cuba's free-trade zones and industrial parks and the employment of foreign staff in mixed enterprises.

Investments are authorized by either the Executive Committee of the Council of Ministers or a government commission designated by the Committee, depending on size, proportion of foreign capital involved, and other factors.

Mixed enterprises enjoy some tax reductions: a tax rate of 30 percent is set on profits, and enterprises pay an 11 percent labor force tax and a 14 percent social security contribution. The free-trade zones offer a liberal tax regime with no duties payable on their imports or exports, and assorted tax holidays. There are no restrictions on the repatriation of foreign partners' profits.

## THE WORKFORCE

For nearly forty years Cubans were guaranteed jobs for life. However, during the Special Period after 1990, the government laid off many workers in the struggle to stave off financial collapse. Opening the doors to self-employment was a response to high unemployment during that period; some have seen the slimming of the civil service as mass redundancy in disguise. Unemployment statistics from Cuba are unavailable, but external sources estimate the unemployment rate in 2004 at 2.5 to 4.1 percent.

### Women in Business

The government's legislation and policy have always supported women's waged employment. According to a government source in 2005, women comprise 45 percent of workers in the civilian state sector, in which they represent

66 percent of all mid- and high-level technicians and professionals. Nonetheless, the glass ceiling is unbroken. Although Cuba is more gender-equal than most Latin American countries, women hold fewer than a third of managerial positions and are underrepresented at the top levels of government.

## UNIONS

The Cuban concept of trade unions is very different from the Western norm. The remodeling of the unions after the Revolution presupposed that in a workers' state the interests of the workers and their employer (the government) were identical, so the unions exist to reinforce government policy and ensure that economic aims are met in the interests of the population as a whole, rather than to defend workers against exploitation. The unions also help to meet certain social needs, but their approach is paternalistic.

The Confederation of Cuban Trade Unions, closely connected to the Communist Party, is the only recognized trade union federation. Independent workers' groups within Cuba report that the government does not recognize independent unions, collective bargaining, or the right to strike, and represses those who campaign for these rights. In April 2003 the International Confederation of Free Trade Unions and other international workers' organizations filed a complaint against the Cuban government with the International Labour Organization (ILO)'s Committee on Freedom of Association. Cuba has ratified the ILO Conventions on freedom of association and collective bargaining, but in 1952, before the Revolution, and the current government has refused to establish a direct contact mission with the ILO.

## THE IMPORTANCE OF PERSONAL RELATIONSHIPS

A good personal relationship is fundamental to a successful business relationship in Cuba, and it is crucial to have an "opposite number" with whom you get along. It's worth remembering that people have both a social and a personal investment in their business relationships. Establishing a climate of goodwill and trust goes a long way to helping a partnership to proceed smoothly.

Such relationships may not be entirely spontaneous, however. In January 2005 the Ministry of Tourism published a code of practice regulating the professional relationships between tourism managers and their foreign counterparts. This has been widely misrepresented outside Cuba as a gag order on staff in tourist establishments; but it is basically a set of directives warning against corruption and promoting efficient, honest, professional relationships. Remember, though, that, however friendly and enthusiastic your contacts may be, they are operating within a controlled and bureaucratic system fraught with ambiguities. The top echelons of the government want foreign business, because only foreign business will save the national economy, but distrust it to some extent because of the social inequalities they fear it may provoke. This may color your business relationships.

## BE PREPARED

Cuba is open for business after decades of isolation from the West, but that doesn't mean Cuban businesspeople are naive. Official statistics are not always reliable, but misinformation about Cuba is rife, and Cubans will be gratified if you have done some homework and are sensitive to their history and culture. Thorough preliminary market research into market niche, partners, and pricing is necessary, and you will need to have established a contact in Cuba before you travel. MINVEC and others can help you to identify appropriate Cuban counterparts. Bear in mind that as the economy improves, the government is becoming more selective about its partners.

It is important to understand that any business contact must go through official channels. You will not be able to arrange a business meeting without contacting MINVEC, the Economic Counselor at the Cuban embassy in your country, and your country's embassy in Cuba. All these contacts are necessary for you to get a business visa, which is also indispensable. These bodies will also brief you about the business environment in general and opportunities in your particular area.

The best initial access point is participation in a trade mission organized by an appropriate institution. The Chamber of Commerce designs tailor-made itineraries for members of trade missions so they get to meet the relevant people in their area. If you participate in a trade mission, you will always meet the Economic Counselor in the Cuban embassy in your country.

Representatives of government entities at a high enough level to be conducting business discussions will probably be able to communicate well in English, but it will be appreciated—and helpful to you—if you know some Spanish.


**MAKING A PROPOSAL**
Once a partnership is identified, the next step is to prepare a proposal to be submitted to MINVEC based on a business plan and feasibility study.

Your chances of success will be enhanced if you can demonstrate that you have a sound medium-term business strategy and the resources and commitment to carry it out. The proposal must be accompanied by documentation such as legal accreditation of the company proposing the association and its representative, and audited financial statements. A draft goes to MINVEC for its recommendations, and once these are agreed upon the proposal is submitted for authorization.

## MEETINGS

Be punctual for meetings. Whatever you may have heard about the Cuban tendency to lateness, you won't create a good impression if *you* are late. The dress code for business meetings is not formal, but women dress more elaborately than men.

Business meetings can vary in style, and are generally cordial and efficient. The degree of protocol involved depends on the level. If a very high-ranking official is involved, they may make a short presentation or speech. One thing that may surprise foreigners is the number of people who attend: it's not unknown for up to thirty people—practically anyone with a connection to the project being discussed—to come to a meeting, though only two or three will speak. This may look inefficient, but promotes transparency.

A smaller meeting will probably start with coffee, or even rum, and icebreaking chat. Business cards will be exchanged. The meeting may take a long time, allowing plenty of time for the participants to get to know each other. It is pointless to try to speed things up. Be patient.

Cubans are very direct in face-to-face communication, and look squarely at their interlocutors. You should maintain eye contact during a conversation, especially in a formal situation.  Looking away may be interpreted as deviousness. If you are making a presentation to several people, look around the room as you talk.

If you host a lunch, it should not be too lavish.

## NEGOTIATING

Don't expect to be able to draw up a finished contract in one or two visits. Since the level of regulation and centralization is very high, there may not be a great deal of room to maneuver in negotiations, but there is evidence that greater flexibility is applied in sectors the government is particularly keen to develop. The chronic shortage of hard currency and the very limited availability of finance are besetting problems for Cuba, so they will bargain hard, but fairly.

It is important to focus on the individuals who will contribute to a decision on your proposal. However, the way to influence them to decide for you is not by lobbying them, as is usual in Europe or North America, but by building up a relationship of personal trust—another reason why doing business in Cuba takes time.

**DECISION MAKING AND FOLLOW-UP**
In state enterprises, decision making is collegiate, almost inevitably involving several levels of government. This is not to say that there won't be a single decision maker at the top who will sign the ultimate authorization (and whose heavy workload may well delay it considerably), but the decision will depend on the gathering and weighing of inputs from many people from ministries and enterprises. How high up the decision goes depends on the size and strategic importance of the project and the divergences of opinion among those who contribute. Although the bureaucracy has lost a lot of weight, it hasn't necessarily become less bureaucratic. Depending on the project, getting from initial approach to approval can take up to twelve months.

At the same time, Cuban enterprises expect replies to their letters, faxes, and telephone calls and may abandon the project if they receive no response. Communications with Cuba are often difficult, but it is vital to keep in touch. Patience and a willingness to keep the relationship—and hence the business—going are fundamental.

## CONTRACTS

Many aspects of the operation of a mixed enterprise are established at the contract stage, and the clearer and more transparent the contract the better. You will need a lawyer who is familiar with Cuban commercial law. You can find an independent lawyer in Cuba, or go through one of the legal practices in Europe that have offices in Cuba and can provide independent advice. Cubans are more legalistic than most, and won't enter legal agreements that are not clear to them. In this sense, they are closer to North American business culture than to Latin American.

Cases of joint ventures being unilaterally suspended should alert potential investors to the need to make sure all contracts contain clear contingency and compensation clauses covering things such as cost overruns, changes in government policy, or other obstacles to delivery.

# chapter nine

# COMMUNICATING

**LANGUAGE**

Although many Cubans speak English, especially in the tourist sector, you will find a little Spanish gets you a long way. Cubans are kindly toward a visitor's efforts, and appreciate those who have taken the trouble to learn their language.

Cuban Spanish is idiosyncratic and the accent notoriously difficult to grasp. It is also spoken very fast (especially in Havana), with a tendency to swallow consonants. You will hear quite a lot of *cubanismos,* such as *guagua* (bus), *jaba* (shopping bag), *quedarse* (to get off, for example, a bus—"*Aquí me quedo*" means "I'm getting off here," not "I'm staying on," which you might expect). Note that *coger* (to get, take) is very commonly used in Cuba whereas in much of South America it is widely used to refer to sexual intercourse. Conversely, don't use *papaya* if you want some pawpaw—in Cuba it means the female sexual organs; a pawpaw is a *frutabomba.*

## WRITTEN COMMUNICATION

The written language is more formal than the spoken language, and indeed can be quite flowery. The general rules for written Spanish apply. As in many other cultures, language in e-mails tends to be less formal and more concise.

Like other Latin Americans, Cubans have two surnames, the father's and the mother's. When a woman marries, she adds her husband's name after "*de*," "*esposa*" (wife) being understood, for example, Rosalía Pérez López [*esposa*] de Gómez; but this final element is used only very formally and to all intents and purposes she keeps her own name, Rosalía Pérez López. Her daughter, however, will be Victoria Gómez Pérez. If a Cuban official writes "SOA" on a form by your name, it means "*sin otro apellido*" (no other surname).

## FORMS OF ADDRESS

Cubans still often call each other—and sometimes foreigners—*compañero* or *compañera*, the revolutionary form of address introduced after 1959. This is not used at the head of a letter, however, especially with someone you don't know well: use *Señor* (Mr.), *Señora* (Mrs.), or *Señorita* (Miss, usually for a young woman). These can be abbreviated to *Sr.*, *Sra.*, *Srta.* "Dear Sir/Madam" is "*Estimado(a) señor(a).*" When speaking, use *señor, señora, señorita* if you're not sure how to address someone. You can use *compañero* or *compañera* for someone you know better. In any case you will soon be on first-name terms. *Señor(a)* is often used as a mark of respect to older people; you may even hear the old-fashioned *don/doña* (with the person's first name, for example, Don José).

In both written and spoken communication, you won't go wrong if you use the formal pronoun *usted* (you) until addressed by the familiar *tú*—but that won't take long, and many Cubans will immediately use *tú*. Once addressed as *tú*, however, don't reply with *usted*—that would come across as a deliberate snub.

**FACE-TO-FACE**
The spoken language is informal and direct, and accompanied by lots of "talking with the hands." If you have been to countries where elaborate and deferential circumlocutions are part of polite speech, Cuban abruptness may raise your eyebrows. For example, there is a tendency to attract your attention or begin a remark with "*Oye*," "Listen!" Where Spanish people answer the phone by saying "*Dígame*," "speak to me," Cubans say "*Oigo*," "I hear you," and they don't always give their names.

Something you may find irritating is the hiss. Saying "*pssst*" to attract someone's attention is not regarded as impolite in Cuba, in fact it's standard practice. You will get used to it!

## Greetings

There are no iron rules, but—particularly in professional settings—men shake hands with each other on meeting, and will usually shake hands with everyone when entering a home or joining a meeting. On first meeting someone, shake hands and say your name simultaneously. Between women, a kiss on the cheek is also a standard greeting, even if you don't know the person very well. This may happen even on first meeting if you have been introduced by a mutual friend. Women, and friends of opposite sexes, tend to greet each other with one or two kisses on the cheek. More kisses will mark your farewells.

## Body Language

Cubans are very tactile, and will touch each other to make a point, be reassuring, express support or sympathy, admire an outfit, and so on. You may see two men apparently arguing vehemently, jabbing at each other with a forefinger; it won't be a quarrel, but probably a discussion of the price of shoes or the baseball results. Heterosexual couples or women friends hold hands in the street, but never two men.

## MEDIA

All areas of the media are state-owned, state-controlled, and tightly censored. The government has never made any secret of its view that the mass media are powerful tools for ideological formation and the development of social consciousness. A foreign editor of *Granma* has said that the role of a revolutionary press is to promote the Revolution, not to criticize it. Thus the information and opinions transmitted are extremely partial. Cuban media produce what the government believes to be socially valuable rather than what will raise the ratings. The absence of advertising is refreshing, even though the alternative is public service broadcasts and revolutionary slogans.

### Television and Radio

There are three national television channels. The main two, Cubavisión and Telerebelde, broadcast a daily news bulletin around midday, and evening programs from 6:00 to 11:00 p.m. (longer on weekends and during July and August). Local stations broadcast before the national programs. A third channel, Canal Educativo, was launched in 2002 as part of the Battle of Ideas (see page 88).

Canal del Sol is a tourist channel, viewable in hotels. Many hotels also have satellite television. For Cubans satellite is not so accessible: though inventive *habaneros* were reported to have made satellite dishes out of old umbrellas, a government clampdown has now made these a rare sight. Many residents of Havana are said to orient their television aerials northward so as to pick up Hispanic-American TV. Public TV programs are published in *Granma*, and Canal del Sol in the business paper *Opciones*.

There are seven national radio stations. Radio Taíno, which broadcasts Cuban and foreign popular music and information about forthcoming events, eateries, and nightspots, is the official tourist station and the one to which most radios in public places are tuned. Most stations broadcast Cuban music, but Radio Musical Nacional specializes in classical music and Radio Reloj has round-the-clock news.

Many people, especially in and around Havana, tune in to radio stations in southern Florida. In 1985 the exile community in Miami set up Radio Martí to beam antisocialist and anti-Castro material at Cuba. The Cuban government tirelessly scrambles the signal, not always successfully. The television equivalent, TV Martí, rarely gets past the jamming signal. Cuba can receive the BBC World Service on shortwave.

## Newspapers and Magazines

Many Cubans are disillusioned with their press. Yet *Granma*, the main national newspaper, and the official organ of the Communist Party, is widely read, and street vendors sell out of it very quickly. A weekly version for foreigners, *Granma Internacional,* is published in English, French, German, Portuguese, and Spanish. It is useful for announcements of developments in commerce and industry, and for those who want to read Castro's speeches in their entirety, but its ceaseless denunciations of U.S. policy can be wearing.

Other daily newspapers are *Trabajadores,* representing the trade unions, and *Juventud Rebelde,* the newspaper of the Young Communists' Union (UJC). Both are in effect versions of *Granma.* There are many provincial newspapers and two weekly business newspapers, *Opciones* and *Negocios en Cuba.* The bilingual cultural weekly *Cartelera* is possibly the most accessible for foreigners.

Magazines include *Bohemia* (cultural and current affairs weekly, founded in 1908), *Prisma* (fortnightly, bilingual, a showcase for revolutionary achievements), *Palante* (humor), and *Revolución y Cultura* and *Gaceta de Cuba* (arts and literature).

Very few international newspapers are available. For foreign publications, look in the Havana hotels Nacional and Meliá Habana. Bookshops sometimes stock back issues of non-Cuban newspapers and magazines.

## TELEPHONE

Some of Cuba's telecommunications are still based on the pre-1959 system. Only local calls can be made from some of the smaller villages, and direct-dialed international calls can be made only to and from Havana. Calls via an operator are subject to delays. However, Cuba is unusual among developing countries in that its telecommunications infrastructure reaches beyond the capital city.

Pay phones are becoming more common. There are three kinds, all operated by the Empresa de Telecomunicaciones de Cuba SA (ETECSA), a joint venture of the Cuban state telephone company and an Italian telecom company. Those that accept the prepaid magnetic phone cards (*tarjetas telefónicas*) sold in post offices, hotels, and other outlets can be used to make direct-dialed international calls.

Local, long distance, and international calls can be made (at a price) from hotels via an operator. Only direct-dialed calls (within Cuba) can be made from a private phone in a house, though direct-dialed international calls can be made on ETECSA phones, found in the homes of most foreigners working in Cuba.

Telex and fax are widely used, and are a good way to book a hotel or a flight or rent a car, since you can keep your own copy.

| Useful Telephone Numbers | |
|---|---|
| **Long-distance call within Cuba from a phone-card public phone** | 0+ area code |
| **Long-distance call via operator** | 00 |
| **Reverse charge international call via operator** | 09 |
| **Direct-dialed international call from a phone-card public phone** | 119 |
| **As above, from a hotel** | 88 |
| **Directory inquiries** | 113 |
| **Police** | 116 |
| **Ambulance** | 114 or 118 |
| **Fire** | 115 |
| Operators may not speak English. | |

## Cell Phones

The current network is aimed at foreign visitors, and coverage is rather weak. The service provider, Cubacel, offers contracts to both visitors and residents, but using a cell phone is expensive. You can try using your own phone, replacing the SIM card with a Cubacel SIM card, but this will not work with all cell phones.

## CUBA AND THE INTERNET

Freedom of Internet communication is a controversial issue in Cuba and a constant topic for the government's critics abroad. Most Cubans do not have personal computers, and although the number of households with online addresses is growing, these are mainly in Havana. Priority is given to government institutions, schools, commercial enterprises, and academics. Cybercafés are rare and mostly located in hotel-based business centers. However, prepaid cards for e-mail and Internet access are increasingly available from ETECSA outlets and can be used in ETECSA offices equipped with computers and Internet access as well as in hotels.

The Internet certainly gives Cubans copious information about their country from the perspective of those who have left it. Even when not published by the exile community and frankly anti-Castro, information about Cuba on the Internet is overwhelmingly from the U.S. or Cuban–American point of view, since information from Cuba itself is both scanty and hard to access reliably.

## MAIL

Post offices keep long hours, often 8:00 a.m. to 10:00 p.m., but even so lines are longest on weekends. Stamps can be bought in hotels as well.

The postal service is generally slow, but posting mail at post offices is said to shorten the delay. All foreign mail has to pass through Havana, and from isolated parts of the island it can take a week to get that far. Mail can take ten days to reach North America and three or four weeks to Europe. Cubans often ask travelers to carry mail overseas to post. The safest and fastest way to post urgent mail, parcels, and documents is via an international courier service.

Cubans still use telegrams widely, and every post office can handle them.

## CONCLUSION

There is greater equality among people in Cuba than in any other Latin American country, and a refreshingly egalitarian mentality that is evident in their friendliness and sociability. One thing that unites them is a steely determination not to allow the United States to own the country again. This is only a part of what makes Cuban society strong. We have also seen the vigor of community spirit, the vitality of local neighborhoods, and the importance of personal and family networks.

Cuba is certainly a country with a clear sense of its own identity and one that inspires strong patriotic emotions in its citizens (and ex-citizens), whatever their political views. The passion, generosity, independence of spirit, and sheer ebullience of the Cuban people are qualities you have to go and experience for yourself.

# Further Reading

This list does not include the many readily available tourist guides. Some of them, such as the *Rough Guide* (2nd ed., 2003) have useful bibliographies.

**History, Politics, Economy**

Carranza Valdes, Julio, et al., trans. and with foreword by Ruth Pearson. *Cuba: Restructuring the Economy—A Contribution to the Debate*. London: Institute of Latin American Studies, University of London, 1996.

Gott, Richard. *Cuba: A New History*. New Haven & London: Yale University Press, 2004.

Guevara, Ernesto, ed. David Deutschmann. *Che Guevara Reader: Writings by Ernesto Che Guevara on Guerrilla Strategy, Politics & Revolution*. Chicago: Ocean Press, 1997.

Marshall, Peter. *Cuba Libre: Breaking the Chains?* London: Gollancz, 1987.

Pérez Sarduy, Pedro, and Jean Stubbs. *Afro-Cuban Voices on Race and Identity in Contemporary Cuba*. Gainesville: University Press of Florida, 2000.

Skierka, Volker. *Fidel Castro: A Biography*. Cambridge and Malden, MA: Polity Press, 2004.

Stubbs, Jean. *Cuba: The Test of Time*. London: Latin America Bureau, 1989.

**Travelogues**

Ferguson, Ted. *Blue Cuban Nights*. Chichester: Summersdale, 2002.

Gébler, Carlo. *Driving through Cuba: An East–West Journey*. London: Abacus, 1991.

Smith, Stephen. *Cuba—The Land of Miracles: A Journey Through Modern Cuba*. London: Abacus, 1998.

**The Arts**

Ades, Dawn. *Art in Latin America*. New Haven & London: Yale University Press, 1989. (Includes several of the best-known Cuban artists.)

Camnitzer, Luis. *New Art of Cuba*. Revised ed. Austin: University of Texas Press, 1993.

Chanan, Michael. *Cuban Cinema*. Minneapolis: University of Minnesota Press, 2004.

Cushing, Lincoln. *¡Revolución! Cuban Poster Art*. San Francisco: Chronicle Books, 2003.

**Language**

*Spanish. A Complete Course*. New York: Living Language, 2005.

*In-Flight Spanish*. New York: Living Language, 2001.

*Fodor's Spanish for Travelers* (CD Package). New York: Living Language, 2005.

**www.afrocubaweb.com** covers Afro-Cuban issues, news, and features on all aspects of Cuban culture, with reviews and announcements of upcoming events in or about Cuba.

# Index

# Acknowledgments

Many people have given me support and information in the writing of this book, but it would not have been possible without the help of Lynn Davie at Aberdeen City Council; David Jessop, director of the Cuba Initiative, London; Emily Morris at the Economist Intelligence Unit; Santiago Pujol, Cuban designer; Dr. Stephen Wilkinson of University College London; and especially my husband, Graham Denyer. My heartfelt thanks to all.